LOCOMOTION PAPERS

The Wrington Vale Light Railway

by
Colin G. Maggs

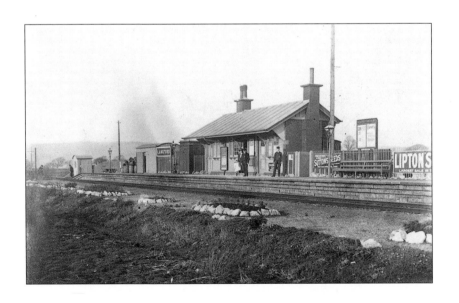

THE OAKWOOD PRESS

British Library Cataloguing in Publication Data
A Record for this book is available from the British Library
ISBN 0 85361 620 5

Typeset by Oakwood Graphics.
Repro by Ford Graphics, Ringwood, Hants.
Printed by Cambrian Printers, Aberystwyth, Ceredigion.

A comic card postmarked 21st March, 1917. *Author's Collection*

Front cover: A hand tinted colour postcard of Langford station *c.*1910
John Alsop Collection

Title page: Langford, viewed towards Wrington *c.*1908. Notice the station building has been extended to the left beyond the chimney stack. Flower beds are between the photographer and the platform. The GWR enticed Langford villagers to be adventurous - the billboard bears posters advertising trips to Cork and Brest. *M.J. Tozer Collection*

Published by The Oakwood Press (Usk), P.O. Box 13, Usk, Mon., NP15 1YS.
E-mail: oakwood-press@dial.pipex.com
Website: www.oakwood-press.dial.pipex.com

Contents

Wrington, looking in the down direction *c.*1904. Coal and coke merchants, Barber Brothers' weighbridge is on the left. A wooden seat stands on the platform.

Author's Collection

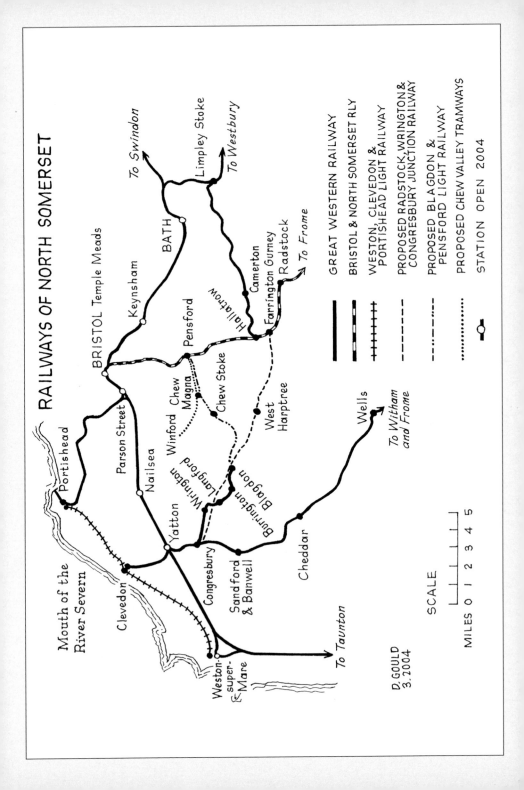

RAILWAYS OF NORTH SOMERSET

Mouth of the River Severn

Portishead

Clevedon

Weston-super-Mare

To Taunton

Parson Street

Nailsea

Yatton

Congresbury

Sandford & Banwell

Cheddar

Wells

To Witham and Frome

BRISTOL Temple Meads

Keynsham

BATH

Pensford

Winford

Chew Magna

Chew Stoke

Wrington

Langford

Burrington

Blagdon

West Harptree

Nailsea

Halatrow

Camerton

Farrington Gurney

Radstock

To Swindon

Limpley Stoke

To Westbury

To Frome

GREAT WESTERN RAILWAY

BRISTOL & NORTH SOMERSET RLY

WESTON, CLEVEDON & PORTISHEAD LIGHT RAILWAY

PROPOSED RADSTOCK, WRINGTON & CONGRESBURY JUNCTION RAILWAY

PROPOSED BLAGDON & PENSFORD LIGHT RAILWAY

PROPOSED CHEW VALLEY TRAMWAYS

STATION OPEN 2004

SCALE

MILES 0 1 2 3 4 5

D. GOULD
3. 2004

Chapter One

Early Railway Schemes
for the Wrington Vale

The Wrington Vale lies approximately midway between Bristol and Weston-super-Mare, snuggling under the north-western slopes of the Mendip Hills. Although Wrington in the centre of the vale was at one time important, it was said jokingly that it was founded in the time of Adam, became a market town during the life of Noah, and has deteriorated ever since. Nevertheless it could boast of two famous residents. The philosopher John Locke (1632-1704), chief figure of the mental awakening which introduced the scientific age, was born there on 29th August, 1632 due to his mother 'travelling in these parts, was here taken in labour, and constrained to take up her residence'. The other was Hannah More (1745-1833), a writer on moral and religious subjects whose work was so popular that during her lifetime her royalties exceeded £30,000 which she left in her will for public and philanthropic purposes. Busts of both these characters may be seen in the south porch of the splendid parish church.

However, Wrington missed out at the start of the railway age, Yatton, four miles distant, being the nearest station when the Bristol & Exeter Railway opened on 14th June, 1841, though the inauguration of the Cheddar Valley line on 3rd August, 1869 brought the railway to Congresbury (variously pronounced 'Congsbry' or 'Coomsbry'), three miles away. Although this partly ameliorated the transport problem of sending the perishable milk, cheese, butter and eggs to market, a line actually running through the vale was really required.

The outlook seemed promising in 1881 when William Adlam, Lord Carlingford, the Hon. Francis Chichester and the Rt Hon. Chichester Fortescue promoted the Radstock, Wrington & Congresbury Junction Railway (RWCJR). A line with great potential, the single line 14¾ miles in length was to run from Farrington Gurney on the Bristol & North Somerset Railway (BNSR) just west of Radstock and pass through West Harptree, Ubley, Blagdon and Wrington to Congresbury where it was to join the Cheddar Valley Railway.

The project had much to be said in its favour. Radstock and Farrington Gurney coal proceeding to markets in South West England would have had a shorter journey than by the existing route through Bristol; opening the line would allow 350 to 374 million tons of coal in seams with an aggregate thickness of 8½ ft to be worked in the field between Chewton Mendip and Nempnett Thrubwell. In fact, in April 1881, a paper read to the South Wales Institute of Engineers by its President, James McMurtrie, revealed that nine-tenths of the course of the proposed line was through a mostly undeveloped coalfield. Additionally the railway would help exploit the ironfield at West Harptree, while a lead mine at Ubley would have been able to increase its output. There was also a lead mine at Redhill. The proposed line would also have have offered railway facilities to 22,000 persons devoid of that method of transport.

Price Williams was appointed Engineer and estimated the cost of the line at £141,000, or only approximately £10,000 per mile compared with the Bristol &

Busts of famous characters born at Wrington: John Locke, philosopher; and Hannah More, moral and religious author; seen here in the south porch of All Saints' church, Wrington, 14th July, 2003.   *Author*

Horse-bus time table Yatton-Wrington from the Bristol & Exeter Railway time table, January 1877.

North Somerset Railway's £25,000. Construction of the RWCJR would have been relatively cheap due to the fact that very few heavy works were required - no tunnels and only 40 yards of rock to be cut through. By April 1882 a contractor had been found willing to raise all the capital and had deposited £7,000 to show his good faith. The RWCJR Bill received the 'hearty support' of the large local landowners, including Lord Carlingford who owned most of the potential coalfield, but it was opposed by the Duke of Cleveland, an absentee landlord who wanted higher compensation than the company was prepared to offer. His opposition increased the cost of obtaining the Bill. The BNSR was also an objector as the proposed line would have siphoned off a significant proportion of its traffic, though James Grierson, General Manager of the GWR, denied that the RWCJR would injure the BNSR which the GWR had agreed to work in perpetuity.

In April 1882 a series of meetings was held in the principal villages in the valley to ascertain the views of residents and it was found that almost all were in favour of the scheme. W.H. Wills of tobacco fame and MP for Bristol, lived at Blagdon and was in favour and the promoters received strong support from the GWR, which on 11th May, 1882 agreed to work the line for 50 per cent of the gross receipts and offer the RWCJR three per cent rebate on all through traffic.

The Commons and Lords Committees were both satisfied from evidence for the necessity of the line. By Act of Parliament 18th August, 1882 a capital of £180,000 in £10 shares, plus borrowing powers of £60,000, was authorized. Unfortunately the contractor proved a man of straw; sufficient capital could not be raised from other sources and the company was dissolved by an Act of 4th June, 1886.

The following year, 1887, another scheme was authorized. The Chew Valley Tramways Company was to construct 6¼ miles of standard gauge steam tramway from the BNSR at Pensford and along the Chew Valley through Chew Magna and Chew Stoke to a terminus at Winford. T.J. Scoones was its Engineer and facilities were to be provided to pick up goods and mineral traffic *en route* and make a junction at Pensford for exchanging traffic. On 25th March, 1887, the scheme came before the House of Lords Committee On Unopposed Bills presided over by the Duke of Buckingham and Chandos and he declared the preamble proved. However, potential backers realised it was not a gold mine and the project was aborted.

Chapter Two

The Wrington Vale Light Railway

As with many abandoned railway schemes, early plans were not entirely forgotten and surfaced later in a shorter proposal. The Light Railways Act of 1896 enabled a railway to be constructed under a Light Railway Order instead of an Act of Parliament, a Light Railway Order being far cheaper and also permitted a line to be more economically constructed by easing normal standards and allowing such things as ungated level crossings and a simpler signalling system.

As a result of local enthusiasm, Colonel Evan H. Llewellyn MP for North Somerset, Sir Edward Hill and others, applied to the Board of Trade in November 1896 for a Light Railway Order to construct a line from Congresbury through Wrington to a terminus at Blagdon from where a short branch would run to the Bristol Waterworks Company's pumping station. This latter line could claim the rare distinction of being a branch, of a branch, of a branch. The course followed by the new railway was almost identical with the western half of the 1882 plan.

Two Light Railway Commissioners, the Earl of Jersey and Colonel Boughey, assisted by a secretary, held a public inquiry at Wrington on 20th May, 1897. Colonel Llewellyn claimed that the proposed line would benefit 14 parishes with a total population of almost 88,000 covering an area of 50 square miles. The population of the major villages was:

Congresbury	1,181
Wrington	1,472
Burrington	400
Blagdon	901

Most of the land was used for dairy farming, so in those pre-refrigeration days, milk, butter and cheese needed to be quickly placed on the market.

Support was given by all relevant parish councils with the exception of Congresbury, which would have gained but little benefit from the project. The Bristol Waterworks Company advocated the line as it was about to construct its Yeo Valley Reservoir and Blagdon pumping station. The GWR, of which Evan Llewellyn became a Director in 1898, undertook, subject to confirmation by its shareholders (whose assent was given in 1899), to finance, construct and work the railway. T.I. Allen, the GWR Superintendent of the Line, commented that he did not anticipate traffic proving remunerative for several years, in fact, initially he expected a loss would be made.

John Russell, the line's Engineer, had been employed by a group of local landowners since the autumn of 1896. He estimated costs at:

	£	s.	d.
Main line	23,071	3	9
Burrington branch to the mouth of Burrington Combe*	1,271	10	0
Blagdon Waterworks branch	648	0	0
Total cost	24,990	13	9

* This branch was never built

Colonel E.H. Llewellyn, a Director of the Great Western Railway and a principal proponent of the Wrington Vale Light Railway.   *Author's Collection*

The steepest gradient on the main line was to be 1 in 50 and the sharpest curve 15 chains (actually 14 chains when built), with only one curve of this radius, the next sharpest having a radius of ¼ mile. Of the nine bridges, six were brick and three steel.

All roads were to be crossed on the level except near Burrington station where an overbridge was required. Some of the public attending the Inquiry pressed for gated level crossings on roads 'with a good deal of traffic' and it was suggested that approaching ungated level crossings a bell be rung on the engine 'but a deaf man might be killed under those circumstances' (laughter). Llewellyn commented:

> As to crossings, we must not expect too complicated and costly arrangements. That's not to say people must not mind being killed now and then, but I feel sure that the Great Western will take every precaution for the safe working of the railway.

After submission to the Board of Trade on 16th November, 1897, the Light Railway Order was confirmed on 18th March, 1898. In addition to a clause conveying the transfer of powers to the GWR, the Light Railway Order included the usual stipulation of a maximum speed of 25 mph (further restricted to 10 mph over ungated level crossings), a minimum rail weight of 60 lb. per yard, a maximum axle load of 14 tons and no gradient steeper than 1 in 50 (or 1 in 30 on the Waterworks branch).

The contract for building the line was let to Herbert Weldon of Birmingham. The summary of costs was:

	£	s.	d.
Fencing - mostly post and galvanised wire	2,849	5	0
Earthwork - excavation of 113,733 cu. yds; embankments 113,670 cu. yds	7,301	13	1
Ballast - some bottom ballast which was stone found in cuttings and broken into 4-6 inch cubes; the rest and top ballast supplied free by GWR	1,980	16	8
Permanent way - laying; packing and boxing up	829	4	6
Culverts and drains	774	10	5
Nine bridges	2,578	17	2
Crossings	992	0	4
Stations - alterations at Congresbury; platforms at Wrington, Langford, Burrington and Blagdon (excluding buildings)	1,143	9	5
Station buildings - new waiting shed at Congresbury and stations at Wrington, Langford, Blagdon and waiting shed at Burrington. (Example of costs: waiting shed £125; station buildings £332 15s. 6d.)	1,829	7	5
Total	20,289	4	0

The contractor was required to take fire insurance on buildings - Congresbury and Burrington £120 each; Wrington, Langford and Blagdon £420 each.

Timber for the fence rails and stakes was to be English oak or larch, and where the timber was creosoted it had to be Baltic redwood. The creosote stipulated was pure coal tar distillate of the very best quality and would be analysed by a GWR chemist

> . . . and if not found satisfactory will be rejected. All gates and posts are to be made from sound, well-seasoned English oak, cut well away from the heart, free from wane [the curved part of tree trunk], shakes [splits], knots and other defects.

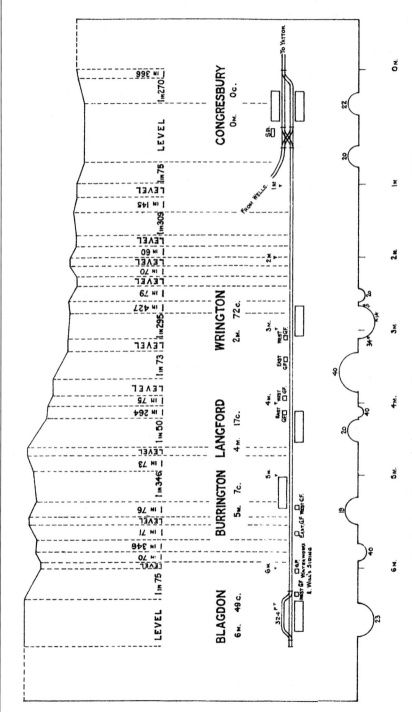

Gradient profile; sketch showing location of ground frames; curvature diagram c.1930.

GREAT WESTERN RAILWAY.

WRINGTON VALE LIGHT RAILWAY.

CONTRACT

FOR

THE CONSTRUCTION OF A RAILWAY

BETWEEN

CONGRESBURY STATION and BLAGDON.

Total Length about 7 Miles.

TENDER.

To THE DIRECTORS OF THE GREAT WESTERN RAILWAY COMPANY.

I, *Herbert Weldon*

of *Norwich Union Chambers, Chamberlain Square, Birmingham* having examined the Drawings and Specification of the above Works, do hereby agree to carry out such Works according to such Drawings and Specification, and upon the terms and conditions therein stated, for the sum of *Twenty thousand two hundred and eighty nine pounds four shillings*   (£ *20,289 : 4 : 0*).

And *I* have in the Schedule hereunto annexed set forth the prices of the different descriptions of work upon which this Tender is based, and according to which additions to or deductions from the Works included in this Tender, as provided by the said Specification, are to be computed; and in case this Tender shall be accepted, *I* hereby undertake to execute a Contract Deed [*and to provide two good and satisfactory Sureties, who, with *me* jointly and severally, will enter into a Bond to the amount of £2,000 conditioned on the due fulfilment of the Contract] or [*by which the Company shall be authorised to retain out of the first or any subsequent moneys payable by them to the Contractor, the sum of £2,000, such retention being in addition to and irrespective of any other moneys authorised by the Contract to be retained or deducted, and to be retained until the certificate in writing has been given by the Engineer, as provided in the Specification, that the whole of the Works have been properly completed].

* The Contractor has an option, and must declare it by striking out the alternative clause.

Witness *my* hand this *thirty first* day of *July* One Thousand Eight Hundred and Ninety-nine.

Herbert Weldon
Assₜ M. Inst. C.E.

First page of the contract for the building the WVLR.

STATEMENT OF CURVES, GRADIENTS, ENGINES USED, AND LOADS OF TRAINS ON THE BRANCH LINES AND LOOPS SPECIFIED.

Branch.	Single or Double Line.	Length.		Maximum Gradient.		Minimum Radius Curve.			Classes of Engines used. Diagram No.	Line and Section of Branch.			Maximum number of Vehicles per Train (including vans.) Loads with two engines (where allowed) shewn in italics.				Number of Vehicles ordinarily run per Train (including vans.) Loads with two engines (where run) shewn in italics.			
				Rising on Up Journey (Falling on Down).	Falling on Up Journey (Rising on Down).	On Rising Grade Up journey (on falling grade Down).	On Falling Grade Up journey (on rising Grade Down).	Minimum radius curve when on Level.			From	To	Coal or Min'ls.	Goods.	Mixed.	Empta.	Coal or Min'ls.	Goods.	Mixed.	Empts.
		M.	Cha.	1 in.	1 in.	Chs.	Chs.	Chs.	See diagrams at end of Statement.	Up or Down.										
Wrington Vale ...	,,	6	41	70	50	18	14	...	28, 40	Up			4	6	6	...	...	...	4	...
										Down			6	9	10	12	...	...	4	...

The "Up Journey" is regarded as in the direction of the junction with the Main or principal line, except where shewn to the contrary.

The maximum loads shewn are for fine weather, and with the class of engine of greatest capacity worked over the branch specified. The assistance of bank engines is understood where stationed and required.

Statement of curves, gradients, engines used and loads of trains on the branch lines and loops specified, 1902.

List of Public Level Crossings

Name of Crossing.	Where Situated between.	Whether a Block Post.	Whether there is a Gatekeeper, Indicators or Bells, if not a Block Post.	Whether there are Signals.	Whether the Gates are Interlocked with the Signals.
Brinsea Road ..	Congresbury and Wrington.	No.	No.	No.	No.
Iwood Lane ..	do.	No.	No.	No.	No.
Wrington ⌐ ..	At end of Station platform.	No.	Gates worked by platform Staff.	No.	No.
Langford	do.	No.	do.	No.	No.
Copthorne Lane ..	Langford and Burrington.	No.	No.	No.	No.,
Bourne Lane ..	do.	No.	No.	No.	No.

Level crossing instructions, March 1910.

Flat-bottomed rail and cattle grids at Brinsea Road level crossing *c.*1923.   *Author's Collection*

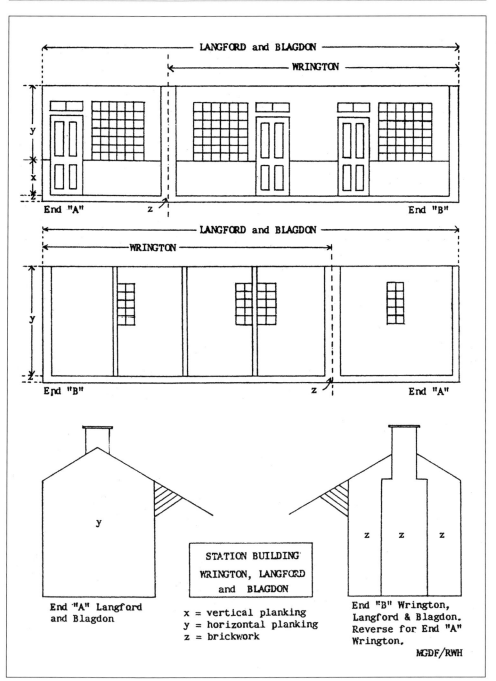

Plan of WVLR station buildings.   *Courtesy Michael Farr*

The gates, posts and ironwork to be painted with two coats of good oil paint after being approved by the Engineer. The butt end of the gate posts to be left unsawn for its whole length, and to be larger in the smallest dimension than the sawn portion.

The iron fencing and gates to platforms will be supplied by the Company in trucks, and the Contractor is to lead [move from point of delivery] unload, distribute and fix the same.

All iron posts are to receive two coats of black varnish, one before being fixed and the other just before the termination of the period of maintenance.

The GWR hired to the contractors 200 tons of bridge rails weighing approximately 62 lb./yd for use on temporary roads, at a cost of four per cent on their value of £4 a ton plus four shillings per ton for transport.

When the ballast is spread, no work whatever shall be carried on over it except the carrying of other ballast, and where this is necessary, every precaution shall be used to prevent the ballast already spread from being trodden down or unnecessarily worked over by horses, or otherwise injured; and in every case, without any exception, where the permanent ballast shall have been injured or shall not be perfectly good, the same shall be removed and replaced by good ballast at the expense of the Contractor.

Road metal was required to be rolled with a heavy steam roller and watered and bound with fine gravel and be four inches thick after the surface had been rolled smooth and firm.

At the commencement of the contract, all permanent way material, supplied to the contractor by the GWR free of cost in wagons, was to be unloaded within 24 hours or a demurrage charge incurred of three shillings per truck per day. Any material damaged after delivery was required to be replaced at the contractor's cost. The faces and soffits of bridge arches were to be faced with one ring of Staffordshire or Cattybrook brindle bricks bonded to the backing rings with similar headers. The mortar was required to consist of one proportion of lime measured dry, and one of sand and one of ashes; the lime to be slaked and thoroughly mixed with the sand, ashes and fresh water under edgestones driven by steam power.

Further specifications:

Cement: one part of best Portland cement to two parts of washed sand.

Masonry: rubble, no ashlar required.

Brickwork: Old English bond.

Stations platforms were to consist of beds of hard, dry filling 6 in. thick, well-rammed and except where paved, to have 4 in. gravel on top, rolled and watered.

The wells at Wrington, Langford and Blagdon to have 3 ft 6 in. internal diameter, 25 ft deep, steined with 9 in. brick, the lower 10 ft laid dry and the upper part built in cement; domed over with half brick in cement with a manhole cover of stone 3 ft x 3 ft and 3 in. thick. Water to be raised by a gun metal semi-rotary pump.

Station damp courses comprised of two layers of slate.

Platform paving (supplied by the GWR): 2 in. thick artificial stone, or a 2 in. thick bed of ashes, bedded and jointed in mortar. To be laid in front of the station building and urinals.

Indication plates supplied by the GWR were: station name boards, on two cast-iron pillars, one to each station.

Small cast iron plates: 'Way Out', one to each station; 'Issue of Tickets, &c', one to each station except Congresbury and Burrington; 'Booking Hall and Waiting Room', one to each station except Congresbury and Burrington; 'Private', one to each station except

Congresbury and Burrington; 'Gentlemen', one to each station except Congresbury and Burrington.

Station roofs were covered with No. 15 Vieille Montagne zinc sheeting 2 ft 8 in. wide. The GWR supplied cast-iron urinals for Congresbury, Wrington, Langford and Blagdon.

The GWR, as owners of the Wrington Vale Light Railway (WVLR), signed and sealed a document on 24th October, 1901 undertaking to work the line with one engine in steam, or two coupled, carrying the single line staff. The Light Railway Commissioners ordered that 'Every engine passing along the Railway should be furnished with a bell or other means approved by the Board of Trade, for giving warning of a train approaching a crossing of any public road on the level'. J.L. Wilkinson, General Manager of the GWR, said that engines were fitted with two whistles, one deep and one shrill, and it appeared to the company that these would be sufficient to meet the requirements. The Board of Trade concurred.

The *Weston Gazette* of 12th October, 1901 announced that construction of the line was almost complete. On Monday 25th November C. Kislingbury, Divisional Superintendent, W.K. Lawrence, Divisional Engineer who had overseen the line's construction, and Frank Morgan, Locomotive Superintendent, left Bristol in the Divisional Engineer's inspection saloon drawn by the locomotive specially dedicated to the WVLR, 2-4-0T No. 1384.* Herbert Weldon, the contractor was also in the party. Although cold and foggy when they set off, the sun shone brilliantly before they reached the Cheddar Valley line at Yatton. The GWR, fully aware of the value of newspaper publicity, invited the press on this trip.

On 28th November, 1901 Lt Colonel H.A. Yorke inspected the improvements at Congresbury and also the WVLR making the following reports:

RAILWAY DEPARTMENT

Board of Trade
8 Richmond Terrace
Whitehall
London, S.W.
Decr. 19 1901

Sir,

I have the honour to report for the information of the Board of Trade, that in compliance with the instructions contained in your Minute of the 28th Nov. I have inspected the alterations at Congresbury station on the Wells branch of the Great Western Railway, which have been carried out in connection with the construction of the Wrington Vale Light Railway.

The works comprise the laying in of a loop line to form a passing place, the building of a new up platform and waiting shed and urinal and the construction of a scissors crossing so as to form a double junction between the existing line to Wells and the new line to Blagdon.

A new signal box has also been erected, and the whole place resignalled. The signal box contains 43 levers, of which 35 are in use, and 8 are spare.

The interlocking is correct and the arrangements satisfactory, and I can recommend the Board of Trade to sanction the use of the new works at this place.

I have etc.
(signed) H.A. Yorke, Lt Col

* See page 87.

RAILWAY DEPARTMENT

Board of Trade
8 Richmond Terrace
Whitehall
London, S.W.
Decr. 19 1901

Sir,

I have the honour to report for the information of the Board of Trade, that in compliance with the instructions contained in your Minute of the 14th Nov, I inspected on the 28th the Wrington Vale Light Railway belonging to the Great Western Ry Company. This line commences by a junction with the Yatton & Wells Branch of the G.W.R. at Congresbury, and terminates at Blagdon. It is single throughout, except at Congresbury, where a short loop forming a double junction with the existing line has been constructed.

The length of the railway is 6 miles 41.24 chains and the gauge is 4 ft 8½ in.

The permanent way is laid with second hand Vignoles rails, except at the commencement where for a length of 7 chains new double headed steel rails weighing 92 lb per yard are employed.

The second hand Vignoles rails are of various sections, but in no case is the present weight less than 65 lb per yard, nor have they lost more than 10 lb per cwt of their original weight.

The double headed rails are supported in chairs, and the Vignoles rails are secured to the sleepers by means of dog spikes and fang bolts. In some cases the fang bolts pass through the flanges of the rails, in others clips are made use of. The line is well sleepered and ballasted, and was in good order, when I saw it.

There are no very steep gradients or sharp curves, the worst inclination being 1 in 50, and the sharpest curve having a radius of 14 chains.

The cuttings and embankments call for no remark.

There are 8 bridges under the line, two of which have wrought iron plate girders below the rails. The girders have sufficient theoretical strength and gave moderate deflections when tested with main line tank engines. The remaining underbridges have brick arches on masonry abutments. There is one bridge carrying a public road over the line; this has steel trough flooring on masonry abutments. All the bridges appeared to be well constructed. There are no viaducts or tunnels.

There are 17 culverts under the line. Mostly of a width of 3 ft or 4 ft. The workmanship in a few of these culverts was of an inferior description. In the case of one culvert, viz that at 1½ miles, the Company agreed to rebuild it before the opening of the line, and orders were given in my presence for this to be done.

There are six public road level crossings, at two of which gates are provided, while at the remaining four there are cattle guards. The conditions laid down in the Light Railway Order have been fully complied with at all these level crossings, and the Company have gone further than necessary under the Order, for the gates are of such dimensions that not only do they fence in the railway when closed across it, but they also fence the road when closed across the latter. The result is that the gates are larger and heavier than would have been the case if they had been made to comply only with Section 16 - sub-section 2(b) of the Order. I understand that the Company designed these gates to meet the wishes of the local authorities.

I noticed 10 sets of field or occupation gates, which were hung so as to open towards the line. These should be altered so as to open towards the adjoining lands in accordance with Sec 68 of the Rly Clauses Consolidation Act of 1845.

There a [*sic*] four stations on the railway viz Wrington, Langford, Burrington and Blagdon. At all of these, single platforms 2 ft high and 200 ft long have been provided. At Wrington, Langford, and Blagdon booking offices, waiting rooms and conveniences for men have been built, and at Burrington there is a shelter.

There are no signals on the light railway except at Congresbury, where there are up home and distant signals worked from the Congresbury signal box, which will be separately reported on.

The line is to be worked by means of one engine in steam, or two engines coupled together, carrying a staff, and I attach the usual undertaking signed by the Chairman and Secretary of the Company to this effect.

There are sidings at Wrington, Langford, and Blagdon stations, and also at an intermediate spot known as 'waterworks siding'. The points at all these places are worked from ground frames, which are locked by the key on the train staff.

At Wrington there are two such ground frames, each containing 2 levers; at Langford two frames each of 2 levers; at waterworks sidings one ground frame containing 4 levers in use and 1 spare lever; and at Blagdon one ground frame containing 4 levers. In all cases the locking is correct and the points provided with the usual safety appliances.

The only requirement noted by me are [sic] in that at Wrington the safety points at the west end of the siding should be altered in position as arranged on the spot.

Subject to this being done within one month, and to the culvert at 1½ miles being rebuilt, I can recommend the Board of Trade to sanction the use of the railway for passenger traffic.

> I have the honour
> (signed) H.A. Yorke
> Lt Col

In the evening of 3rd December, 1901 the Great Western Directors and William Dean travelled over the line. Perhaps this rather strange time was chosen because afterwards they were guests of Sir W.H. Wills at Coombe Lodge, Blagdon, so probably dined with him.

The branch opened to the public on Wednesday 4th December, 1901, the first train from Blagdon, its coaches comfortably filled, arriving at Wrington on time and leaving to waves of coloured handkerchiefs. The Wrington porter beamed because there was no luggage and the station master had a haggard appearance 'caused no doubt by overwork'. The three-coach set was insufficient to handle traffic on the first day and required strengthening.

The *Clevedon Mercury* reporter captured the excitement felt at Wrington:

Long before this hour [8.14 am the arrival time of the first train] a crowd of villagers had assembled at the station, a great many of them booking to intermediate stations down the line. All through the day could be seen streams of people going to the station to have their first trip, every train being crowded. Several firms closed for the day, and gave their workpeople free tickets to go where they chose. Many of them made a trip to Blagdon, and took the opportunity of looking over the pumping station and waterworks. The Revd G.M. Ashdown also took the Wrington choir boys to Blagdon. Flags were hoisted in the village, and everything passed off most successfully.

All children in the district were granted a holiday, while those at Blagdon were to be treated to a free ride to Burrington, a villager offering to defray expenses. When the GWR heard about it, they offered free travel. On the opening day scholars assembled at the school, marched to the station, stopping *en route* at Mr Wood's shop where they were given sweetmeats. They proceeded on to the station where they travelled by special train as all the regular first day trains were crowded. About 1,500 passengers travelled on the first day.

GREAT WESTERN RAILWAY.

OPENING

OF THE

WRINGTON VALE

LIGHT RAILWAY.

On WEDNESDAY, DECEMBER 4th, 1901,

This Line will be opened for Public traffic with Stations at

WRINGTON, LANGFORD, BURRINGTON

AND

BLAGDON.

DOWN TRAINS.		WEEK DAYS ONLY.				UP TRAINS			WEEK DAYS ONLY			
		A.M.	A.M.	A.M.	P.M.				A.M.	A.M.	P.M.	P.M.
London (Paddington)	dep.		7 25	11 45	3 0	BLAGDON	dep.	8 0	9 35	2 35	5 20
Bristol (Temp. Meads)	,,	8 5	11 20	3 25	6 10	Burrington	,,	8 4	9 39	2 39	5 24
Yatton	arr.	8 33	11 40	3 45	6 38	Langford	,,	8 8	9 43	2 43	5 30
						Wrington	,,	8 14	9 49	2 49	5 40
Taunton	dep.		9 43	1 35	4 48	Congresbury	arr.	8 23	9 58	2 58	5 55
Weston super Mare	,,	7 45	10 54	3 25	6 0						
Yatton	arr.	8 4	11 7	3 39	6 13	Congresbury	dep.		10 0	3 40	5 1
						Axbridge	arr.		10 20	4 0	6 20
Clevedon	dep.	7 55	10 50	3 12	6 0	Wells	,,		10 50	4 30	6 50
Yatton	arr.	8 3	10 58	3 20	6 8						
						Congresbury	dep.	8 24	9 59	2 59	6 0
		A.M.	A.M.	P.M.	P.M.	YATTON	arr.	8 30	10 5	3 5	6 7
YATTON	dep.	8 40	11 50	3 50	6 50						
Congresbury	arr.	8 43	11 54	3 53	6 53	Yatton	dep.	8 58	10 25	3 37	6 32
						Clevedon	arr.	9 6	10 33	3 45	6 40
Wells	dep.	7 20	9 50	2 15	4 55						
Axbridge	,,	7 48	10 22	2 48	5 30	Yatton	dep.	8 33	11 1	3 29	6 26
Congresbury	arr.	8 4	10 42	3 8	5 50	Weston super Mare	arr.	8 52	11 25	3 45	6 40
						Taunton	,,	10 13	12 47	5 43	8 55
Congresbury	dep.	8 44	12 0	3 54	6 54						
Wrington	,,	8 52	12 11	4 2	7 2	Yatton	dep.	8 37	10 19	3 39	6 13
Langford	,,	8 59	12 23	4 9	7 9	Bristol (Temp. Meads)	arr.	9 6	10 50	4 0	6 35
Burrington	,,	9 5	12 34	4 15	7 15	London (Paddington)	,,	12 55	2 40	7 0	10 10
BLAGDON	arr.	9 10	12 40	4 20	7 20						

Passengers, Parcels and Goods traffic will be dealt with at Wrington, Langford and Blagdon, and Passengers only at Burrington.

PADDINGTON, November, 1901.   **J. L. WILKINSON, General Manager.**

WYMAN & SONS, Ltd., Printers, 63, Carter Lane, Doctors Commons, E.C.   (1366a)

A poster time table for the opening of the Wrington Vale Light Railway, Wednesday 4th December, 1901.
Author's Collection

Coombe Lodge, Blagdon, formerly the home of Sir W.H. Wills, 14th July, 2003. *Author*

Wrington station and part of the Vale seen from the tower of All Saints' church in 1905. The passenger platform is centre right and the goods yard centre left. *Author's Collection*

On 4th December Sir W.H. Wills, champion of the new line, entertained local dignitaries at Coombe Lodge after they had ridden over the line. He was reported as saying that he believed that the opening of the line would do a lot for Blagdon, for they would be able to leave at eight o'clock in the morning and be in Bristol by nine o'clock, which he knew would suit his agricultural friends very well, especially on Thursdays (market day in Bristol). And if their wives wanted to go to Bristol with their produce, they would be able to get there long before the ladies of Clifton got down to the city.

He could not help thinking that Blagdon was not going to take a back seat; the land offered opportunities for building that would be very attractive to the people of Bristol and the fishing in the district was, he believed, some of the best in England.

The day following the opening, an unfortunate accident occurred to George Brooks, a labourer cutting large limbs from a tree overhanging the railway at Wrington. One of the boughs splintered and threw him from the ladder to the ground. He was carried home and a doctor fetched. Several ribs were broken and his shoulders painful.

Lord Winterstoke, as Sir W.H. Wills later became, owned a farm at Devizes and periodically returned from Wiltshire on the last train to Blagdon in a first class compartment.

When the Scottish entertainer Will Fyffe (1884-1947) fished at Blagdon Reservoir, he lodged at Blagdon with guard Albert Jones.

Pre-World War I schools closed for a week for blackberry-picking in order to augment a family's near subsistence income. Labourers' wives and children picked all day. Mr Poultney of Congresbury supplied chip baskets to the pickers. A considerable number of filled baskets were dispatched by train.

The railway was useful to the community apart from providing transport. Not everyone could afford a radio to set the correct time, but could rely on the local station clock which was checked by telephone at 9.00 am each day. The phone installed at stations and signal boxes was often used to spread national news faster than newspapers were able to do.

A quiet time at Blagdon, viewed towards the stop blocks c.1923.   *Author's Collection*

Chapter Three

Description of the Line

Wrington Vale branch passenger trains usually started at Yatton in order to avoid a troublesome double change for main line passengers. The Blagdon branch itself left the Cheddar Valley line at Congresbury, situated 15 ft above sea level. Hitherto Congresbury had a single platform, but then its junction status required a passing loop.

The original substantial standard Bristol & Exeter Railway building, dating from 3rd August, 1869, of Mendip stone, with decorative roof tiles, cruciform ridge tiles and intricate barge boards, had a single platform set on the east side of the line. The up platform had a timber waiting shelter with bay windows and a brick-built chimney. No footbridge was provided, passengers using a sleeper crossing to reach it.

At the south end of the down platform was a standard Bristol & Exeter stone-built goods shed containing a 2 ton crane with a 12 ft 6 in. radius swing. Near the goods shed was a cattle loading dock. The new up platform road, twoloop lines south of the station; an up goods siding and a new signal box were brought into use on 14th April, 1901 eight months prior to the opening of the WVLR. Left of the goods yard entrance was a weighbridge and weigh house. Wagons for coal merchant Bill Gill (or Harold Harvey from 1935) were left on the stop block of the Back Road. A short siding leading from the weigh bridge road was lifted by May 1930.

With greater numbers of people taking holidays in the 1930s, coupled with an expansion of interest in camping and walking, led to a 6-berth camp coach being placed at the station 1935-1939. Its occupants criticised its position at the end of the Shed Road and close to the Back Road where coal was unloaded, so when the camp coach was restored post-war 1952-1962, it was placed on No. 2 up siding which offered a more attractive situation, but was further from the station toilets and drinking water. Coach No. W9901 was used in 1959 and 1962. A coach provided everything campers required and had a waterproof advantage over a tent. The local station master suggested places to visit in the locality and the railway fares of camp coach users were often substantially greater than the coach hire charge. A porter cleaned the coach after the occupants left and checked that nothing had been stolen which required paying for; he also filled the lamps with oil.

In 1915 the staff at Congresbury consisted of five, but by 10th March, 1921 comprised the station master, two signalmen, and three porters. Two of the latter worked early and late duties in alternate weeks and took charge during the station master's absence, also attending to goods yard work including shunting. The third porter assisted with office work and relieved other porters. His chief office work was booking milk and parcels traffic, entering invoices and assisting with monthly goods and parcels accounts.

In the 1930s, staff consisted of the station master, two porters and two signalmen. It was in this era that the station master's house (still standing today)

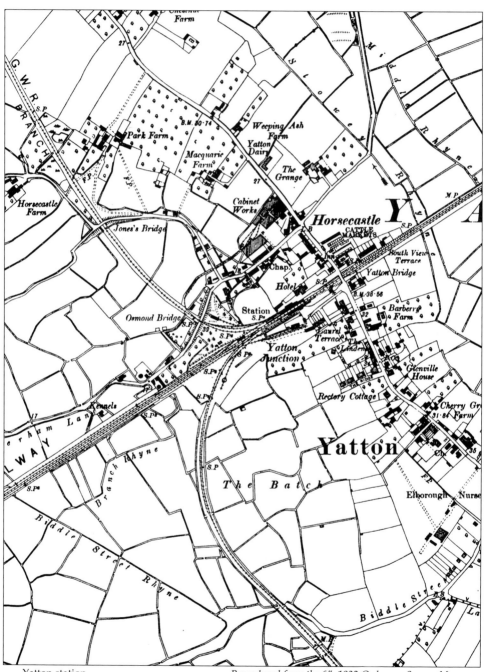

Yatton station.

Reproduced from the 6", 1932 Ordnance Survey Map

Great Western Railway Station, Yatton.

The south end of Yatton station viewed from the signal box *c.*1904. The branch train in the down bay platform may be for Wrington. *Author's Collection*

Passenger trains at all four Yatton platforms *c.*1908. A Dean 'Single' heads the down main line train. *Author's Collection*

'4575' class 2-6-2T No. 5528 approaches Congresbury with the 7.58 am Yatton-Witham on 13th
June, 1957.   *Author*

Renewing the bridge across the River Yeo immediately north of Congresbury station.
                                                                  Author's Collection

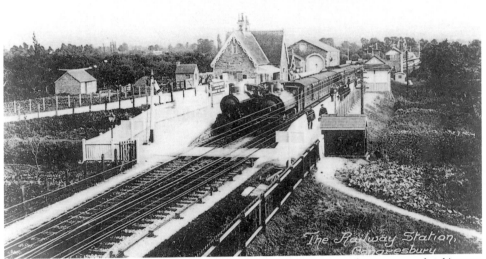

An 0-6-0ST heading an up passenger train at Congresbury *c.*1904, overtakes an up goods taking refuge on the down line. The station nameboard reads 'Congresbury Junction for Wrington Vale Branch' A coal merchant's small cabin is to the left of the station building. A railwayman's allotment is on the right behind the up platform. *Author's Collection*

Congresbury station garden and staff *c.*1915. The weighbridge hut is in the right background. *Author's Collection*

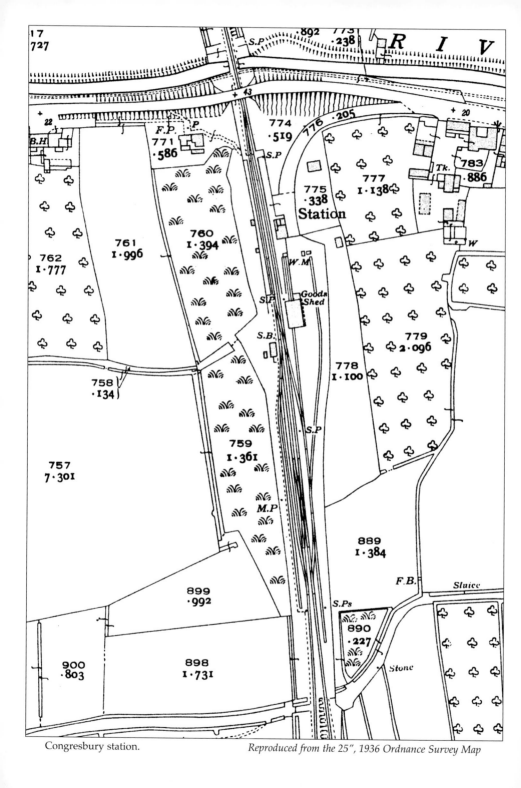

Congresbury station.

Reproduced from the 25", 1936 Ordnance Survey Map

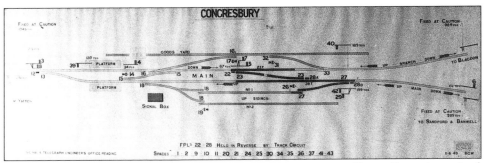

Above: Congresbury signal box diagram, dated 11th June, 1949. *Author's Collection*

Left: Exchanging tablets at Congresbury: '51XX' class 2-6-2T No. 4103 leading, and '61XX' class 2-6-2T No. 6148 as train engine, with the Home Counties Railway Society's special. The signal arm has been pulled off for the Cheddar Valley line, 6th October, 1963. *R.E. Toop*

Below: Congresbury signal box in 1954.
M.J. Tozer Collection

Congresbury, view in the up direction in 1954. Notice the decorative window frames of the goods shed.   *M.J. Tozer Collection*

A down view at Congresbury on 27th August, 1954. The small shed on the far right held the Wrington ganger's velocipede. The Wrington branch curves left in the distance.   *Author*

Congresbury, view in the up direction in 1954. *M.J. Tozer Collection*

Congresbury, view looking down in 1954, showing the up platform and bay-windowed waiting shelter added for the WVLR. *M.J. Tozer Collection*

Ex-GWR diesel railcar No. 24 at Congresbury working a Yatton-Witham service in 1954. Signalman Bob Ford returns to his box with the Yatton-Congresbury tablet.   *M.J. Tozer Collection*

The approach drive to Congresbury station; the gates to the goods yard and the shed beyond, 1954.   *M.J. Tozer Collection*

Congresbury goods shed, 1954. Notice the loading gauge suspended from a bar above the doorway.   *M.J. Tozer Collection*

Congresbury goods shed in May 1968. Inside on the right can be seen brackets for holding the fire buckets.   *D.J. Hyde*

Congresbury on 11th March, 1961: class '2' 2-6-2T No. 41208 with the 1.27 pm Yatton-Wells, crosses '57XX' class 0-6-0PT No. 8746 heading an up goods. The bridge in the background carried the Bristol-Weston-super-Mare main road. The 'B' class headlamp on the buffer beam was unorthodox, but frequently practised on the GWR and the WR. *R.E. Toop*

The next three photographs form a sequence at Congresbury on 22nd October, 1962. 10.20 am: and Ivatt class '2' 2-6-2T No. 41208 (82E, Bristol, Barrow Road) approaches with a train of empty ballast hoppers for Sandford & Banwell. Normally these were worked by the Cheddar Valley goods, but on this date it had been delayed and so the quarry wagons were taken by the Wrington engine before it returned to Congresbury to work the branch goods. Part of the Camp Coach may be seen on the far right. *Author*

10.30 am: '57XX' class 0-6-0PT No. 3696, minus its shed plate, arrives with a Cheddar Valley goods. *Author*

11.15 am: No. 41208 leaves with the Wrington goods. The Cheddar Valley line is on the left. Notice the World War II concrete pot-type sleepers with tie-bars. *Author*

A goods train from Wrington headed by '58XX' class 0-4-2T No. 5809 approaches Congresbury on 31st August, 1950.   *D.W. Winkworth*

A Camp Coach on No. 2 siding, Congresbury in 1954. The Wrington branch is straight ahead, while the Cheddar Valley line curves right.   *M.J. Tozer Collection*

was built near the A370. The station buildings were demolished in October 1968. A short distance to the west is the rather concealed entrance to the Cheddar Valley Walk, the path passing between the platforms (still extant and now sheltered by a canopy of trees). The station closed to passengers on 9th September, 1963 and to goods on 1st July, 1964. North of the station the River Yeo was crossed by an iron girder bridge of 23 ft 6 in. span, renewed shortly before closure.

The Blagdon branch left the Cheddar Valley line 8 chains from the station and curved south-east. Brinsea Road (1 mile 10 chains from Congresbury) was the first of the ungated level crossings with cattle grids to prevent animals straying along the railway. A 1901 report described the feature:

> On each side of the crossing a shallow pit has been dug underneath and at right angles with the line of rails. Over the top of this opening iron bars are placed in the form of a grating. It is found from experience that animals do not venture across an arrangement of this kind, which is therefore, known as a cattle 'fence'.

The crossing provided three warnings to users: a notice bearing the words 'Beware of Trains'; then the standard warning sign of a stylised picture of a locomotive with the words 'Crossing No Gates' below and a red triangle; and finally a large notice 'Trains Cross Here' with reflecting lenses to show clearly after dark and having a small red triangle on top. The latter sign was the responsibility of the railway, but the others were erected by the local highways authority. This crossing is just about traceable today.

The first recorded accident at an ungated level crossing on the WVLR occurred on 23rd September, 1919 when a motor cyclist from Wrington, at Brinsea Road crossing struck the buffer beam of the locomotive working the 6.45 pm Yatton to Blagdon passenger train and was killed outright. At the inquest, the locomotive driver, Reginald Fletcher of Blagdon, said that he reduced his speed from 20 mph to 10 mph before the crossing and sounded his whistle. His statement was corroborated by another witness who added that all engine drivers were most careful at crossings, in fact their whistling was 'somewhat of a nuisance'. The motor cyclist's speed was estimated at 40-50 mph. Following the accident, the train stopped within 100 yards.

During World War II one United States' general infantryman riding a motor cycle, when he heard the engine's whistle, believed he could beat the locomotive and accelerated. Discovering he could not cross before the train, he braked heavily and skidded into a wet, muddy ditch.

What was probably the final accident on a WVLR crossing occurred exactly 33 years to the day after the first. A 3 ton South Western Electricity Board lorry travelling towards Congresbury, collided with an engine at Brinsea Road crossing on 23rd September, 1952. The lorry was overturned by the locomotive. The lorry driver was unharmed, but a passenger beside him was thrown through the cab window and needed treatment at Weston hospital as did a passenger in the rear of the lorry who was thrown across and received minor injuries. Driver Sidney Sledge stopped his engine, two goods goods wagons and a brake van about 100 yards beyond the crossing. He, his fireman and guard were unhurt. The engine only had a length of vacuum pipe torn from its front and several rivets broken.

'14XX' class 0-4-2T No. 1412 at Brinsea Road level crossing on 13th June, 1957. It lacks smokebox plates showing its number and shed. Note that all three wagons are of timber construction.

Author

'58XX' class 0-4-2T No. 5813, still bearing 'GWR' on its side tanks on Iwood Lane level crossing on 27th August, 1954.

Author

Flat-bottomed track and cattle grid at Iwood Lane level crossing on 27th August, 1954.   *Author*

Ivatt class '2' 2-6-2T No. 41208 'engine and brake' at Iwood Lane level crossing *en route* from Wrington to Congresbury on 22nd October, 1962.   *Author*

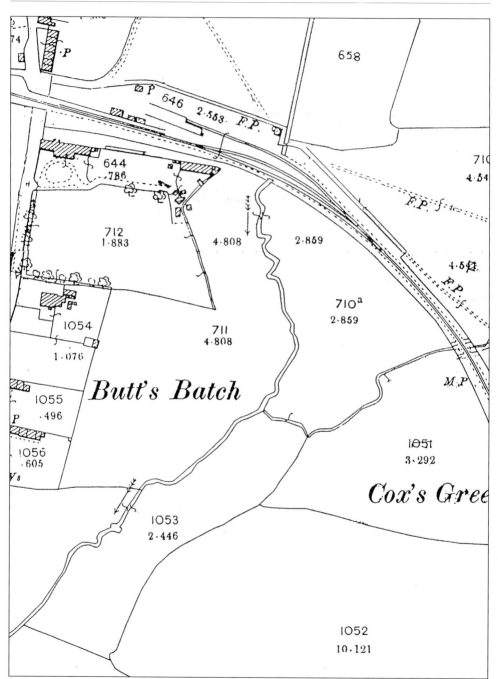

Wrington.   *Reproduced from the 25", 1903 Ordnance Survey Map*

Three-quarters of a mile beyond Brinsea Road, the line crossed Iwood Lane (1 mile 67 chains), a similar crossing and provided with the same safeguards. The site of the crossing is still fairly obvious today. Five hundred yards east of Iwood Lane was a 14 ft span girder bridge over the River Yeo.

Between Congresbury and Wrington the line undulated, varying from level to 16 chains of 1 in 60, but usually the gradients were only of short duration, the tendency being to rise.

Wrington station (2 miles 64 chains), was on the east side of the gated crossing over Station Road, the gates being of fairly intricate design. The station building was of timber and red pressed brick, its zinc roof extended beyond the eaves to form a canopy over the bay windows and part of the platform. Adjacent was a standard GWR cast-iron gentlemen's urinal and a corrugated iron parcels shed.

Beyond the passenger station was a goods loop and siding, the former controlled by Wrington West ground frame (2 miles 66 chains), and Wrington East ground frame (2 miles 74 chains), worked either by the station master or porter. The yard had a 30 cwt hand-operated crane - the only one on the branch and installed some time after 1904. There was also a horse and carriage dock.

Industry at Wrington consisted of Organ Brothers, upholstery manufacturers and saddlers, some flock arriving in sheeted open wagons from Bristol and some from Exeter; that from the latter source was disliked by the station master and porter as it was dirty - after handling it, they went home with fleas. Saddles and bridles were dispatched by passenger train. Horse collars were wrapped in hessian bales. Six to eight milk churns left daily. Milk contracts included a clause that the farmer, or his employee, was required to assist the station staff load full churns and unload the empties. Each 17 gallon churn weighed 2¼ cwt when full.

Incoming traffic consisted of coal - in the 1950s Messrs Clements received an average of three wagons daily. Other traffic was flour for Lynham's the bakers who collected it by horse and cart. Grain arrived for Walters, millers. Animal feedstuffs such as cattle cake and sugar beet pulp arrived for farmers. Wrington, like the other branch passenger stations, closed to passengers on 14th September, 1931, while the goods yard, latterly dealing only with full wagon loads of coal, closed on 10th June, 1963, but the weighbridge and office remained in use as a coal office until the 1980s. The station site now forms part of the housing estate 'Old Station House'.

In April 1902 Wrington was staffed by a station master and lad porter, this number still being on the books in 1916. On 4th February, 1921 staff consisted of a station master, porter, lad porter and charwoman. The lad porter cleaned and trimmed all lamps, assisted with general station duties and, using sack trucks, delivered parcels within ½ mile radius.

In 1950, after closure of the line from Wrington to Blagdon, the branch ended in buffer stops 19 chains beyond the passenger platform.

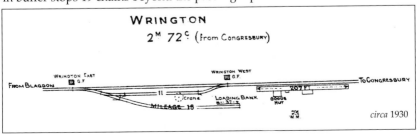

circa 1930

'58XX' class 0-4-2T No. 5813 and brake van approaching Wrington on 27th August, 1954. Cows in the background pass over an occupation crossing as the engine waits for Station Road level crossing gates to be opened.   *Author*

Ivatt class '2' 2-6-2T No. 41208 waiting for Station Road level crossing gates to be opened on 22nd October, 1962. The houses on the right have been erected since the previous photograph was taken.   *Author*

The substantial Station Road crossing gates *c.*1905. Notice the wicket gate for pedestrian use after the main gates have been closed. A large Great Western Railway billboard adjoins the left-hand gate. *Author's Collection*

A solid-tyred lorry stands in the station approach near the coal office and weighbridge in the late 1920s. On the platform are parcels and a milk churn. A box van is near the yard crane. *Author's Collection*

The goods yard at Wrington *c.*1941 with the passenger station beyond. To centre right is the cattle dock. The Ford lorry has a masked headlight and the location name on the cab door is painted out in compliance with wartime regulations.   *M.E.J. Deane*

'3571' class 0-4-2T No. 3573 at Wrington and the 1½ ton crane.   *M.E.J. Deane*

Bells on arrival at Wrington in 1911 in GWR 4-plank open wagon No. 701. They were destined for All Saints' church and dispatched from Mears' Bell Foundry, London. Six had been retuned and four were new. *Miss V. Perry Collection*

'58XX' class 0-4-2T No. 5813 shunting at Wrington, 27th August, 1954. Note the 'Restricted User' brake van. The 1½ ton crane is worked by pulling a continuous chain. *Author*

Wrington station, view down, 2nd April, 1950.   *Grahame Farr*

Wrington station, view to crossing gates *c.*1960.   *Lens of Sutton*

Details of the platform side of Wrington station building, 1962, with the Great Western Railway cast-iron notice still attached. *Michael Farr*

The rear of Wrington station building, 1962. *Michael Farr*

The modified weighbridge house, Wrington, 1962.   *Michael Farr*

Corrugated iron parcels lock-up, Wrington, 1962.   *Michael Farr*

A '14XX' class 0-4-2T from Yatton shed shunts the daily freight in Wrington yard on 1st September, 1953, while W.E. Clements' lorry is loaded with coal direct from wagons.
Michael Farr

Ivatt class '2' 2-6-2T No. 41208 shunts at Wrington on 22nd October, 1962, view looking down. Coal merchants were prohibited from propping wagon doors when unloading due to the danger of the prop being dislodged and coal falling on workmen. *Author*

Ivatt 2-6-2T No. 41208 shunting at Wrington, near the stop blocks on 22nd October, 1962. A pile of concrete pot-type sleepers is on the right.   *Author*

One of the few underbridges on the WVLR. Photographed on 14th July, 2003 it is situated to the east of Wrington, it has stone abutments, a blue brick arch with stonework above.   *Author*

The line curved sharply on a 14 chain radius curve and re-crossed the River Yeo via a steel bridge. It was not unknown for train crews to come armed with rods to fish for trout. The line crossed a drive over a stone and engineering brick bridge which still stands as do the medium height embankments on either side.

The line climbed at 1 in 73/75 to Langford (4 miles 9 chains), where the passenger station was similar to that at Wrington, but with an extra room added at the north end *circa* 1908 offering three doors to the platform instead of two. Also on the platform were a cast-iron gentlemen's urinal and a corrugated-iron parcels lock-up, while at the foot of the western ramp was an oil store. As there was no room for flower beds on the platform, they were situated on the far side of the track. Although the building was demolished in 1958, the platform and level crossing gate could be seen until recently.

The goods loop and siding with carriage dock, immediately west of the passenger platform, were controlled from Langford West ground frame (4 miles 0 chains), and Langford East ground frame (4 miles 6 chains), both worked by the station master. Coal merchants using the yard were Messrs Clements and Messrs Cole, while during and after World War II, often seven to eight wagons of scrap metal arrived with Central Supply Depot equipment such as United States' Army Jeeps broken into scrap. These wagons were unloaded by Italian prisoners-of-war who caught sparrows and made them into soup. If there was insufficient space in the sidings at Langford, wagons were held at Congresbury.

Another World War II activity at Langford was sack repair, Bernard J. Downey having converted piggeries into the more delightful-sounding Pear Tree Works. Including those for his depot at Blagdon, the branch carried annually 75,000 sacks, each weighing 3½-4 lb., and an average of three wagons for Langford or Blagdon arrived from Bristol each day. Langford closed to goods on 1st November, 1950. A camp coach had been available at Langford in the 1930s.

Col E.H. Llewellyn lived at Langford Court. He was a principal instigator of the WVLR and a Director of the Great Western Railway 1898-1914. 4-4-0 No. 3419 (re-numbered 3367 in 1912) was named *Evan Llewellyn* after him, while 4-6-0 No. 2946 was named *Langford Court*. Following education at Rugby School, he trained as an engineer on the London & North Western Railway.

'Bulldog' class 4-4-0 No. 3367 *Evan Llewellyn* at Reading, 2nd October, 1926.
Colin Roberts Collection

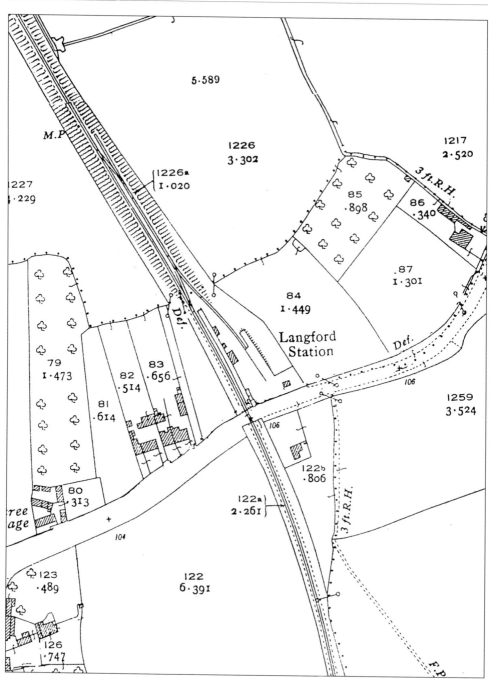

5·589

M.P

1226
3·302

1226a
1·020

227
·229

1217
2·520

3 ft. R.H.

85
·898

86
·340

·87
1·301

84
1·449

Def.

Langford
Station

Def.

106

79
1·473

82
·514

83
·656

81
·614

1259
3·524

80
3·313

106

122b
·806

122a
2·261

3 ft. R.H.

ree
age

104

123
·489

122
6·391

126
·747

F.P.

Langford.

Reproduced from the 25″, 1929 Ordnance Survey Map

LANGFORD

4^M 17^C

circa 1930

Langford station, view down *c*.1910. A cast-iron gentlemen's urinal is left of the station building. The latter originally had two doors, but was extended to the left. Milk churns and barrels are on the platform. The station master's house may be seen on the far side of the gated level crossing.
Author's Collection

Langford, view up *c*.1903. The station building is on its original condition with just two bay windows. In the distance to the left is the goods yard and loading gauge. Note the gradient post in the lower left-hand corner - 1 in 244 down (*to the left*) and 1 in 50 up (*to the right*).
M.J. Tozer Collection

Langford station, view up, 2nd April, 1950. Notice the sheeted wagons and a box van on the siding beyond the station building.   *Grahame Farr*

The attractive level crossing gate at Langford on the north side of the road.   *Lens of Sutton*

'58XX' class 0-4-2T No. 5809 at Langford: fireman George Hunt on the running plate; an unidentified Bristol driver and guard Bert Maslen, right, *c.*1950. *Author's Collection*

Station staff at Langford in 1902 comprised the station master and a lad porter, while 1916 saw two staff still employed there. On 4th March, 1921 a survey reported that although traffic had been affected by road competition, no corresponding reduction in staff could be made because two were required to cover the hours of train service. The station master was withdrawn on 29th December, 1925 and, when the country lorry service was introduced in the 1930s, the post of porter was abolished and the Wrington porter travelled on the train to Langford to attend to the crossing gates. In 1953 when the A38 was widened, land near the level crossing was conveyed free to the Somerset County Council. The Western Region estimated the cost of track removal at £15 and the cost of not having to maintain the roadway, the removal of a gate and fencing off the new boundary, would save £15 per annum. The former station master's house (erected in 1903 at a cost of £372) on the south side of the crossing is still extant, but so altered as to be almost unrecognisable as having railway origins.

From Langford the line climbed at 1 in 50 for ¾ mile passing Copthorn Lane ungated crossing (4 miles 64 chains), over a lane unmetalled to this day. It reached the summit 160 ft above sea level just before Burrington station. This gradient sorely taxed the Clevedon branch steam railmotor (*see Chapter Five*), sometimes causing it to run out of steam, while in the freight-only era, driver Fred Flower, or his colleague 'Ginger' Parsons, ran ahead of the engine pouring sand on the rails to improve adhesion. For up goods and mixed trains, a Stop Board was placed near the 4¾ mile post which required brakes to be pinned down to control the descent to Langford.

Just prior to entering Burrington station (4 miles 79 chains) was a cutting through hard limestone conglomerate. This cutting was subject to drifting snow and, on at least one occasion, a fireman stood on the buffer beam, held his

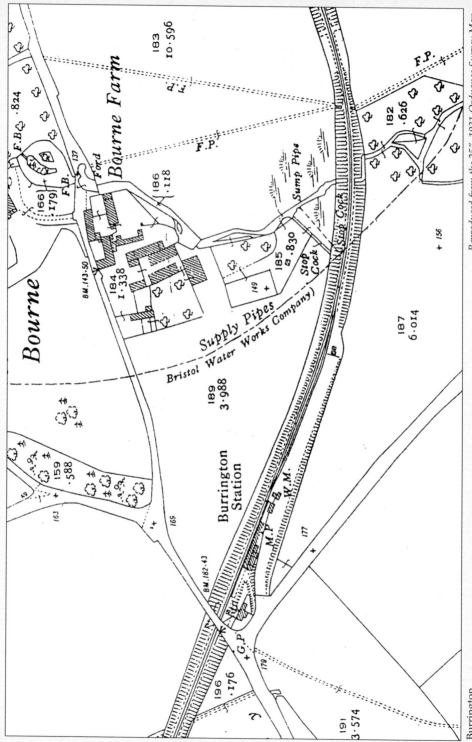

Burrington.

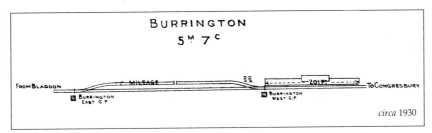

BURRINGTON

5ᴹ 7ᶜ

FROM BLAGDON ← MILEAGE → 201 FT TO CONGRESBURY
BURRINGTON EAST G.F.
BURRINGTON WEST G.F.

circa 1930

shovel down and hit the snow from the rails. In autumn this cutting accumulated leaves which caused slipping. The cutting was spanned by a steel girder road bridge which was the only one on the branch. In the 1980s it required a £10,000 repair and so was demolished and the cutting in-filled.

The original Burrington station, nearly a mile from the village, was simply an open shelter, identical to that on the up platform at Congresbury, passengers obtaining tickets from the guard, but a stone station building with timber canopy was brought into use on 26th September, 1907. There was also a luggage store, weighing machine and oil store. One of the station's regular users was a boy who travelled daily from Yatton to do a paper round at Burrington. The station was demolished in 1958, but the station master's house still stands. The station was set about a mile from the picturesque Burrington Combe where the Vicar of Burrington 1762-1764, the Revd Augustus Toplady, composed the hymn *Rock of Ages*, and even after the line had closed to regular passenger traffic, one excursion was run from Bristol to Burrington carrying pilgrims.

Initially Burrington had no accommodation for freight, but a goods loop was brought into use on 2nd July, 1903 with Burrington West ground frame (5 miles 1 chain), and Burrington East ground frame (5 miles 6 chains), together with a weighbridge in the station yard. A corrugated iron goods shed was provided in addition to a horse and carriage dock. During World War II as many as 10 wagons of timber would arrive for safe storage at Churchill Rocks, well away from German incendiary bombs. The station closed to goods on 1st November, 1950, but the station house still stands. The staff of one in 1916 had risen by 4th March, 1921 to station master and porter.

Beyond Burrington a short rise was followed by a fall at 1 in 70 for about half a mile, passing Bourne Lane ungated level crossing (5 miles 33 chains), just east of the hamlet of Bourne. East of the crossing site ballast is still visible and about 150 yds from the lane is an occupation crossing and quarter mile post formed of bridge rail and a wood backing for the figures, but the '5½' is missing.

The line rose at 1 in 75 through the scenic Rickford Valley to reach the terminus at Blagdon (6 miles 37 chains), and 152 ft above sea level. At 6 miles 1 chain were two ground frames. That on the left controlled a siding that descended at 1 in 65 to Bristol Waterworks' Yeo pumping station, GWR tracks terminating at gates across two sidings (6 miles 23 chains). An employee recalls that wagons were drawn up this gradient by a hand-powered winch. Beyond the gates, each track split into two to serve the pumping station. The siding was provided under an agreement of 24th November, 1902 and was terminated on 30th September, 1940. The siding actually came into use in January 1904 and was lifted in July 1941.

The neat, stone-built station at Burrington, with the station master, right, and porter, left, c.1920. Notice the array of poster boards attached to the building; also the corrugated iron goods shed beyond.   *D. Lovelock*

Burrington, view up on 2nd April, 1950. Notice the stone station building.   *Grahame Farr*

'3571' class 0-4-2T No. 3573 at Burrington c.1941; guard Bert Maslen stands with his shunting pole. The driver is 'Doctor' Day. *M.E.J. Deane*

'3571' class 0-4-2T No. 3573 shunting at Burrington c.1941 with a storm sheet roughly folded on top of the cab. *M.E.J. Deane*

Burrington station, viewed in the down direction on 19th August, 1954. Notice that the far end of the platform is raised.   *Author*

The former station master's house at Burrington beside the A368 on 14th July, 2003.   *Author*

The site of Bourne Lane ungated level crossing on 14th July, 2003. The modern gate is supported by a length of bridge rail, while a GWR concrete post can be seen to the left.   *Author*

A length of bridge rail forming the support of the 5½ mile post 150 yards east of Bourne Lane level crossing, 14th July, 2003.   *Author*

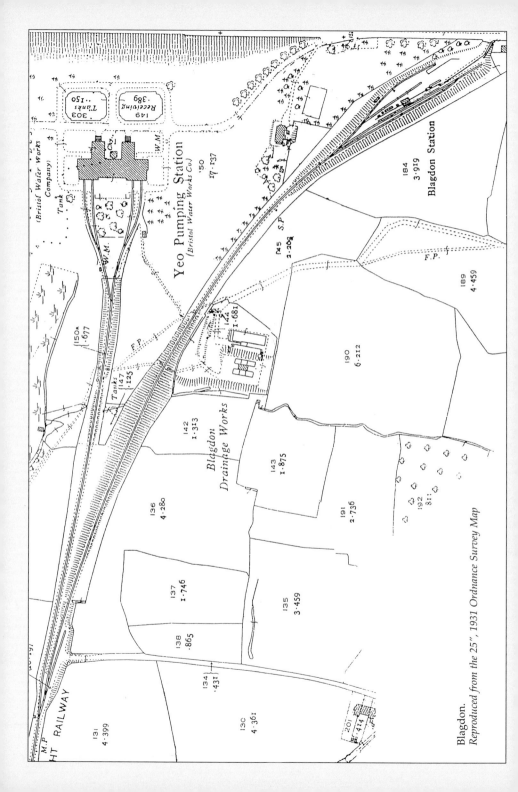

Yeo Pumping Station
(Bristol Water Works Co.)

(Bristol Water Works Company)

Blagdon Station

Blagdon Drainage Works

HT RAILWAY
M.P.

303 Tanks ·150

149 Receiving ·389

·50
17·137

184
3·919

189
4·459

190
6·212

143
1·875

191
2·736

192
81·

142
1·313

136
4·280

137
1·746

138
·865

135
3·459

134
·431

130
4·361

131
4·309

201
·414

150a
·677

147
·125

144
1·681

F.P.

F.P.

S.P.

145
2·204

Tank

Tanks

W.M.

W.M.

W.M.

Chy.

Blagdon.
Reproduced from the 25″, 1931 Ordnance Survey Map

The story is told that normally coal wagons had grease axle boxes, but one day a wagon with oil boxes arrived and ran so freely that it broke through the power house door. Some coal from the pumping station came from Pensford & Bromley Colliery - a distance of 27½ miles by rail compared with only 10 miles by road, which was probably why, at some period prior to 1925, coal was indeed conveyed by road, though fortunately later returned to rail.

The 260 ft long siding to the right was Wills' (or Lays Lane) Siding, a short line for use by Sir W.H. Wills' Coombe Lodge estate and its noted shire horses. The siding agreement was made on 2nd July, 1901 and ended on an undetermined date. The GWR had the privilege of shunting engines and rolling stock into this siding if room was available and could also use his road for access by GWR servants, but not the public. His road descended on a gradient of 1 in 6½ to the siding. No surcharge was made for the use of the siding, the rates being as to or from Blagdon.

Blagdon station building was similar to those at Wrington and Langford, but with an extra room added at the west end *circa* 1908 making three doors on to the platform instead of two. A run-round loop was beside the platform road, with the stop block at 6 miles 41 chains. Blagdon West ground frame was at 6 miles 31 chains, and Blagdon East ground frame, 6 miles 39 chains. The station was unfortunately inconveniently located about half a mile from the village and 200 ft below it.

There were two mileage sidings, a water pump and stables. During World War I Granny Filer knew not when to expect her son back from the front, so the driver alerted her by three extra toots on the whistle. On Saturdays, the evening train brought the sporting newspapers, the 'pink 'un' and the 'green 'un'. The young Sampsons and Carpenters waited to meet the train and start selling the papers. Visitors came by train to the Mendip Bungalow and Nordrach Sanatorium. The former was purpose-built as an hotel. It had asbestos walls and a corrugated iron roof - several other houses in the neighbourhood also had this form of construction.

Figures show that in June 1928 just 100 parcels arrived and 14 were dispatched; also there were two churns of milk night and morning and eight trucks of coal for the waterworks. Prior to the introduction of the country lorry service with driver Bill Hodder, a van of 'smalls' traffic conveyed parcels between Yatton and Blagdon.

Occasionally an unusual train arrived at Blagdon. The arrival of a new Rector of Butcombe passed into local legend, for he stylishly arrived in a special train carrying his family, servants, household goods and all the family animals. In 1948 a farmer, his livestock and deadstock arrived by train from Maidenhead when moving to Nempnett Thrubwell, the final 2½ miles having to be completed by road. The end-loading carriage dock proved useful on this occasion.

Sacks became very important traffic on the branch during World War II. Bernard J. Downey started life as a sack trader with horse and cart at St Philip's Marsh, Bristol. He expanded his business and sent sacks to the eastern counties and Scotland. His trade developed even more and he exported to Ireland, Holland and Belgium. He also imported cotton sugar bag liners from the USA.

In December 1940, needing a larger home, he purchased The Close, near Blagdon church. Sacks were vital to the war effort. Besides the need for sand bags to protect people and buildings from blast damage, they were required by the Ministry of Supply's Port Area Grain Committee; the Home Grown Cereals Division; the Potato Division, etc.

Blagdon, December 1901: wagons belonging to John Wainwright & Co., Moors Hill Quarry, Cranmore, on the left behind the platform; beyond are short-wheelbase wagons, some unsprung, of Herbert Weldon, the railway contractor, awaiting removal. The Inspection House, used by the supervising Bristol Waterworks Engineer, stands high in a commanding position.

Author's Collection

Blagdon staff on the platform *c*.1910. The '517' class 0-4-2T has a train of at least four coaches - the three-coach branch set plus a six-wheeler. The second coach has a white patch around a window where a temporary repair has been made. The corrugated-iron lock-up is on the right. The Waterworks' pumping station chimney can be seen above the railway station building.

Author's Collection

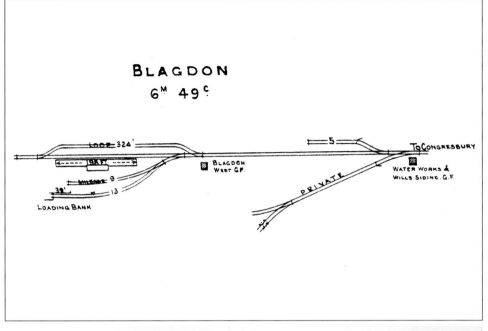

Blagdon on 22nd August, 1937 with the Camp Coach in the siding; the grounded coach used as a porters' room and the water pump column on the far left. *A.R. Ball*

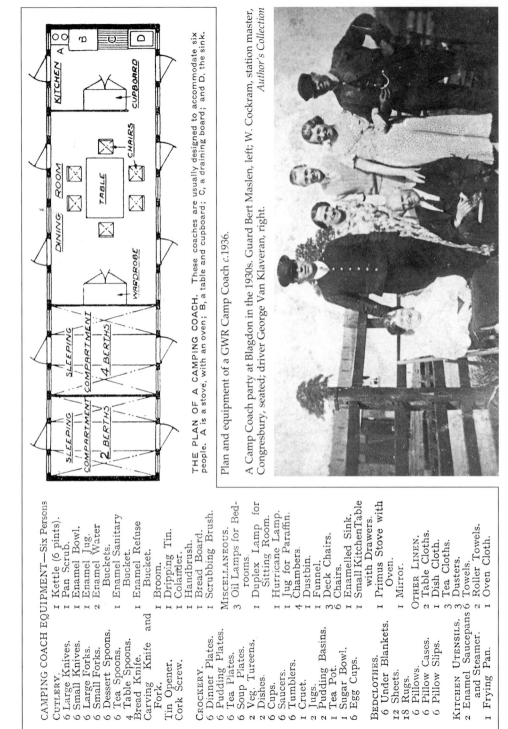

THE PLAN OF A CAMPING COACH. These coaches are usually designed to accommodate six people. A is a stove, with an oven; B, a table and cupboard; C, a draining board; and D, the sink.

Plan and equipment of a GWR Camp Coach c.1936.

A Camp Coach party at Blagdon in the 1930s. Guard Bert Maslen, left; W. Cockram, station master, Congresbury, seated; driver George Van Klaveran, right.
Author's Collection

CAMPING COACH EQUIPMENT—Six Persons

CUTLERY.
6 Large Knives.
6 Small Knives.
6 Large Forks.
6 Small Forks.
6 Dessert Spoons.
6 Tea Spoons.
4 Table Spoons.
Bread Knife, and Carving Knife and Fork.
Tin Opener.
Cork Screw.

CROCKERY.
6 Dinner Plates.
6 Pudding Plates.
6 Tea Plates.
6 Soup Plates.
2 Veg. Tureens.
2 Dishes.
6 Cups.
6 Saucers.
6 Tumblers.
1 Cruet.
2 Jugs.
2 Pudding Basins.
1 Tea Pot.
1 Sugar Bowl.
6 Egg Cups.

BEDCLOTHES.
6 Under Blankets.
12 Sheets.
18 Rugs.
6 Pillows.
6 Pillow Cases.
6 Pillow Slips.

KITCHEN UTENSILS.
2 Enamel Saucepans and Steamer.
1 Frying Pan.
1 Kettle (6 pints).
1 Pan Scrub.
1 Enamel Bowl.
1 Enamel Jug.
2 Enamel Water Buckets.
1 Enamel Sanitary Bucket.
1 Enamel Refuse Bucket.
1 Broom.
1 Dripping Tin.
1 Colander.
1 Handbrush.
1 Bread Board.
1 Scrubbing Brush.

MISCELLANEOUS.
3 Oil Lamps for Bedrooms.
1 Duplex Lamp for Sitting Room.
1 Hurricane Lamp.
1 Jug for Paraffin.
4 Chambers.
1 Dustbin.
1 Funnel.
3 Deck Chairs.
6 Chairs.
1 Enamelled Sink.
1 Small Kitchen Table with Drawers.
1 Primus Stove with Oven.
1 Mirror.

OTHER LINEN.
2 Table Cloths.
1 Dish Cloth.
3 Tea Cloths.
3 Dusters.
6 Towels.
2 Roller Towels.
1 Oven Cloth.

A view of Blagdon station *c*.1903 before it was extended towards the camera. A cast-iron gentlemen's urinal is in the centre of the picture and a milk churn. The grounded coach body, part of which may be seen, contained stables in the eastern half, while the porters' room occupied the remainder. The roofs of the branch passenger set can just be seen above the grounded body's roof. The locomotive run-round loop is in the foreground. *Author's Collection*

Soon after moving to Blagdon, he obtained permission to store jute sacks, before they were processed elsewhere, in the redundant Blagdon station waiting room, ticket office and other buildings. Not long after, due to bomb damage to his premises at Bristol, he started sack cleaning and repair in the disused stables at The Rectory, next door to his house, the Rector agreeing to a 7½ hp vacuum cleaner being installed. Later Downey obtained premises at Langford. At Blagdon the train crew often played football with his girl employees.

A six-berth camp coach was placed at Blagdon in 1935 and, as passenger traffic had ceased by this date, campers were advised to travel by bus. Their linen arrived from the GWR laundry, Swindon, in a wicker hamper carried by passenger train to Yatton and then onwards to Blagdon in the goods guard's van, together with lamp oil. Also in the guard's van the Wrington porter brought fresh water from Congresbury to the coach daily.

In 1902 the Blagdon station master was paid £1 7s. 0d. per week, the porter 17s. and the branch guard £1 1s. 0d. The number of staff in 1916 still numbered three. On 10th March, 1921 the complement was: station master, guard, porter-guard and porter. The porter-guard worked the 4.55 pm Blagdon to Yatton and the 6.45 pm Yatton to Blagdon, the remainder of his time spent relieving the porter for meals, etc. He was also responsible for cleaning the branch passenger train. When Albert Maslen was porter-guard at Blagdon in the 1920s, he reported to the station master at 9.00 am and tidied the station. He worked the Waterworks ground frame and then walked to Burrington and tidied up there before returning to Blagdon for a two-hour break before his afternoon shift when he took over from regular guard Albert Jones.

The station closed to goods on 1st November, 1950 and the building was later converted into a private house.

Blagdon in 1948, viewed in the up direction.   *Grahame Farr*

The building at Blagdon on 27th August, 1954 following track lifting.   *Author*

Re-birth: Blagdon station sensitively converted into a home, view west *c.*1963. *Lens of Sutton*

Blagdon view east *c.*1963. *Lens of Sutton*

CONGRESBURY.

Shunting on the Wrington Vale Line while the Train Staff is at Blagdon.

For the purpose of Shunting the Down Goods Siding at Congresbury Station whilst the Train Staff is at Blagdon, Engines with or without trucks may run on to the Wrington Line, but such permission is given on the distinct understanding that such occupation of the Wrington Line must be carried out before 7.30 a.m. and not before it has been ascertained by telephone that the last Train for the day has arrived at Blagdon.

With Down Trains while the Engine with or without trucks runs on to the Wrington Line the rear part of the Down Train must stand on the Down Line at the Platform.

Shunting on to the Wrington Line, except as herein provided, must not be carried out unless the Staff is at Congresbury Station.

WRINGTON VALE BRANCH—Working of Goods Traffic.

It is important that Mixed Trains should be delayed as little as possible in dealing with Goods Traffic, and, as a rule trucks must only be shunted off into the Loop or Siding.

An Engine and Goods Van with local traffic will leave Blagdon daily for Wrington or Congresbury, as shewn in Working Time Table, for the purpose of Shunting the Sidings at Burrington, Langford and Wrington, and placing outwards traffic into position for the Mixed Train Blagdon to Congresbury and for working traffic to and from Stations between Wrington, Langford, Burrington, and Blagdon in both directions.

Mixed Trains will be worked in accordance with the Standard Regulations shewn in the General Appendix to the Book of Rules and Regulations.

Traffic to and from the Wrington Line must be dealt with at Congresbury Station and worked to and from that Station by Goods Trains for and from the Cheddar Valley Branch.

Occupation of the Wrington Vale Line by the Permanent Way Department.

1. The Engineering Department will have absolute occupation of the Line between Congresbury Inner Home Signal on the Wrington Vale Line and Blagdon from 5.0 a.m. daily (Sundays included) until 15 minutes before the first Train is due to leave Blagdon. If any work is taken in hand during that interval and it cannot be completed, or a Trolley is on the Line, and will not be removed 15 minutes before the first Train is due to leave Blagdon, the Ganger must act in accordance with Rules 248, 250, and 251 of the Book of Rules and Regulations, and also telephone to the nearest Station in the direction from which the Train is due. In such a case the Train must be stopped and detained at that Station until the Ganger advises the Station Master, by Telephone or otherwise, that the Line is clear.

2. No Special Train must be run during the time the Engineers have absolute occupation in the early morning (see clause 1) unless written notice has been previously given to the Ganger, and his receipt is held for it. Occupation of the Branch by the Engineering Department after the Train service for the day has been completed and up to 5.0 a.m. must only be arranged under special instructions from the Divisional Superintendent. In any case of emergency between these times the Ganger must send out Flagmen in accordance with Rules 248, 250, and 251 of the Book of Rules and Regulations. If it should be necessary to run a Special Train over the Branch without notice during the daytime from either Congresbury or Blagdon, each Station Master must be advised by telephone and an acknowledgment received before the Special is run.

3. To obviate the necessity for sending out Flagmen in accordance with Rules 248, 250 and 251, of the Book of Rules and Regulations, when it is necessary to run Trolleys along the Line or to carry out operations (except as shown in Clause 1) which would render the running of Trains unsafe, telephones for the use of the Ganger to communicate with either of the Stations on the line are fixed in Huts at the following points, and the instructions shewn below must be strictly carried out :—

Places where Telephones are fixed, giving Distance from Congresbury.			Station to be Telephoned to.	
Nos. of Huts and Mileage from Congresbury.		Between.	For Up Trains.	For Down Trains.
	Miles. Chns.			
Hut No. 1	75	Congresbury and Wrington ...	Wrington	Congresbury.
„ 2	1 70	„ „ ...	„	„
„ 3	3 36½	Wrington and Langford	Langford	Wrington.
„ 4	6 1	Burrington and Blagdon (at Junction of Will's Siding)	Blagdon	Burrington.

NOTE.—Telephones are also provided at the following Stations :—Congresbury, Wrington, Langford, Burrington and Blagdon

4. The Telephonic Code Calls for the various Stations on the Line are as follows :—

	Congresbury.	Wrington.	Langford.	Burrington.	Blagdon.
No. of Rings :	2	3	4	5	6

Appendix to the Service Time Table, March 1910: working of goods traffic and occupation of the WVLR by the permanent way department.

Signalling and Permanent Way

Signalling on the branch was simple: at Congresbury a fixed distant, outer and inner home, and at Blagdon a fixed distant warning the approaching end of the line.

In due course a notice was issued that

> From 2nd April to 20th April, 1928, between the hours of 9.0 am and 4.0 pm daily (Sundays excepted) yellow lights and arms will be brought into use in place of existing red lights and arms in all distant signals from Yatton, Cranmore and Blagdon. The District Inspector concerned to make the necessary arrangements for safe working in accordance with Rule 71.

The Signal & Telegraph Department, Taunton District, was responsible for the Blagdon branch.

The line was worked on the 'one engine in steam' principle with Annett's key attached to the wooden train staff for unlocking ground frames at the intermediate stations. An omnibus telephone circuit linked all the booking offices and telephones were also provided in the platelayers' huts.

The original rails lasted in most places for the life of the branch. These Vignoles flat-bottomed rails were spiked directly to the sleepers. One spike was knocked in on each side of the rail, but alternative sleepers had one spike on the outside only. To counteract rail creep, bullhead rails in chairs replaced Vignoles on the 1 in 50 between Langford and Burrington, while *circa* 1950 the track just west of Wrington was relaid with bullhead rail in chairs. In places, chairs were secured to World War II concrete pot-type sleepers.

The Wrington Vale branch was the second line to have the GWR's 'Economic system of track maintenance'. This 1903 innovation permitted a permanent way gang to have total possession of the line during a long gap in the train service. With this system no flagman or look-out was required because the telephone circuit along the branch was used by the ganger in charge of the work, to call the signalman and obtain permission to obstruct the line at a specific location for an agreed length of time.

The permanent way gang, believed to consist of a ganger, sub-ganger and about eight men, stationed at Wrington had charge of the whole branch and used a pump trolley. Latterly the line was maintained from Congresbury.

In passenger train days the Engineering Department had occupation from 5.00 am until 15 minutes before the first train was due to leave Blagdon, while in post-World War II times they had occupation from 5.00 am until 15 minutes before the first train was due to leave Congresbury and from 15 minutes after it had returned there.

On one occasion a guard had orders to learn the road to Blagdon. Arriving at Congresbury by passenger train, he found that the daily freight to Blagdon had already left, so set off on foot. Arriving at Wrington he had seen no sign of the train and was horrified to observe that the permanent way men had removed a rail. He advised the ganger to replace the rail quickly before the train returned and received the reply that it had returned to Congresbury while he, the ganger, was having breakfast. The guard, on foot, commented that what the ganger had really heard was its departure for Blagdon, not Congresbury.

Blagdon c.1930: porter Arthur Cockram, right, with his father standing in the van, and the guard, left.
Author's Collection

Engine Whistles

STATIONS AND JUNCTIONS.	Whistles.	REMARKS.
CONGRESBURY—		
Main	1	
Branch	2	
BRINSEA ROAD CROSSING ..	1	
(Between Congresbury and Wrington)		Drivers to give one
IWOOD LANE CROSSING ..	1	long whis-
(Between Congresbury and Wrington)		tle when approach-
WRINGTON STATION	1	ing these
LANGFORD STATION ...	1	Crossings
COPTHORN LANE CROSSING ..	1	on the
(Between Burrington and Blagdon)		Wrington Vale
BOURNE LANE CROSSING ..	1	Railway.
(Between Burrington and Blagdon)		

NOTE.—At Level Crossings and other places are fixed, Drivers must give one long whistle. in connection with which " Whistling Boards "

Instructions for whistling, March 1910

Railway enthusiasts at Iwood Lane ungated level crossing c.1959. Note the flat-bottomed track. Ivatt class '2' No. 41208 approaches with a goods train comprising two coal wagons.

M.E.J. Deane

Engine Restrictions

Branches

Section of Line	Route Colour	Engines Authorised	Local Prohibitions
Wrington Branch	" Uncoloured "	" Uncoloured," B.R. Standard Class 2 (2–6–0) and ex-L.M.R. 2–6–2T (412XX).	Congresbury: B.R. Standard, Class 4 (4–6–0) and 78XX Classes not to work into Goods Shed Road.

Engine restrictions, extract from Working Time Table, 9th June to 14th September, 1958.

The guard set off at a brisk pace towards Blagdon, hoping to be able to warn the crew. He reached the 14 chain curve east of Wrington when the goods approached.

Until the last few seconds he stood in the middle of the track with both arms raised and as the 0-4-2T passed, bellowed to the fireman 'Rail out!', and pointed towards Wrington. He shouted the same message to the guard.

He waited for the sound of the crash, but none came, so made his way to Blagdon.

Later he discovered what had happened. The labourers had over-ruled their ganger and restored the rail just before the train arrived.

On 1st July, 1949 the scissors crossing at the south end of the Congresbury layout, and an unnecessary expense since the withdrawal of the Blagdon branch passenger service, was replaced by a slip connection in front of the signal box. Points were normally set for Congresbury goods yard which acted as trap points for any branch runaways.

In October 1960 the only crane permitted on the branch was the 45 ton crane belonging to the Chief Mechanical & Electrical Engineer's Department, Swindon, the Bristol cranes being too heavy.

No. 41208 passes Iwood Lane crossing with a goods c.1959. Note the type of fencing.
M.E.J. Deane

Chapter Four

Events Leading to Closure

As happened with so many railways opened late, closure was early, at least, regarding passenger services. As early as 4th February, 1921 it was revealed that traffic at Wrington was adversely affected by road transport, but no reduction could be made in the number of staff employed there. It was the same story the following month at Langford. Traffic had declined due to road competition, but no compensating reduction in staff could be made because two men were required to cover the hours of the train service. It is significant that in July 1921 the Burrington stop of the 6.45 pm ex-Yatton was made conditional. Similarly at Blagdon, in March 1921 it was found that passenger and parcels traffic had decreased due to road competition, two bus services running daily from Blagdon to Bristol. It was not surprising that passengers deserted the railway, for it was both quicker and cheaper to travel 11 miles by bus rather than 19¾ miles by rail and involving a change of train. Stabling the branch train and locomotive at Yatton was considered, but deemed as offering no saving to the Traffic Department, though in fact, this step was taken from 31st March, 1924. Traffic had also declined at Burrington in 1920 'and the chief reason is road competition' - but again, no reduction in staff could be made.

Declining revenue warranted a close inspection of the branch on 11th November, 1925. The train service over 11½ hours daily was worked by two sets of enginemen from Yatton. Although the passenger traffic was light, apart from one steam railmotor each way daily, the economy of railmotors could not be introduced because the loading, working and shunting restrictions imposed on these units precluded the services from being entirely worked by them.

In 1925 the average numbers of wagons daily on the branch were:

Coal & Minerals		General Goods		Milk Churns	No. of Livestock
Forwarded	Received	Forwarded	Received	per annum	trucks per annum
-	4	2	6	12,841	44

Broken down into stations figures were:

	In	Out	
Wrington	3	1	
Langford	1	1	
Burrington	1	1	(per week)
Blagdon	2	1	

Most inwards traffic was coal; milk traffic was considered 'good' and general goods were conveyed in the station truck. It was proposed to economise by concentrating all the branch clerical and accounts work at Wrington and make the station master there responsible for the other branch stations which would be solely manned by porters. This would offer an annual saving of £245. The station houses at Langford, Burrington and Blagdon would then be occupied by the respective porters. The station masters were withdrawn on 5th January, 1926.

Report on the WVLR, 1925

EXPENDITURE

			£	Percentage of traffic receipts
Traffic Department Staff - Paybill Figures				
Station	*1924*	*1925*		
Wrington	319	315		
Langford	221	209		
Burrington	224	208		
Blagdon	277	199		
Junction staff	293	294		
	£1,334	£1,225		
		Total	1,225	19.77
Loco. Department, Engine & Train Running Expenses				
Coaching	£1,888			
Freight	£575			
		Total	2,463	39.75
Engineering Department, Maintenance & Renewal			1,790	28.89
Signal Department, Maintenance & Renewal			164	2.64
Clothing			36	.58
Fuel, lighting, water and general stores			25	.40
Rates			143	2.30
		Total	£5,846	94.33

Goods Tonnage, forwarded and received 1925

Coal & Minerals	4,868	12,481 cans of milk (by passenger train)
General Goods	2,711	44 trucks of livestock (by goods train)

Daily average of wagons dealt with:

Coal & Minerals	Forwarded 0	Received 4
General Goods	Forwarded 2	Received 6

RECEIPTS

Station	Passenger	Parcels	Goods	1925 Total	1924 Total	Increase or Decrease
	£	£	£	£	£	£
Wrington	465	451	1,602	2,518	2,610	-92
Langford	134	565	376	1,075	1,142	-67
Burrington	211	616	627	1,454	1,545	-91
Blagdon	386	256	506	1,148	1,118	+30
		Total	£6,195	£6,415		-£220

Proposed Alterations: Replacement of Station Master by Porters, except at Wrington where Branch Accounts and Clerical Work are concentrated. Estimated Annual Value of Savings £245.

Left: Steam railmotor No. 38 and driver at Blagdon.
M.E.J. Deane Collection

Below: The last passenger train from Blagdon on 12th September, 1931: driver Arthur Jones, fireman Frank Salter and guard Bert Maslen. Notice the low platform. *Author's Collection*

TRAFFIC DEALT WITH AT STATIONS.

STATION	YEAR	Staff No. (Supervisory & Wages, all Grades)	Paybill Expenses £	TOTAL RECEIPTS £	Tickets Issued No.	Season Tickets No.	Passengers Season (incl. Tickets, etc.) £	Parcels £	Miscellaneous £	Passenger Total £	Fwd. Coal & Coke "Charged" Tons	Fwd. Other Minerals Tons	Fwd. General Merchandise Tons	Recvd. Coal & Coke "Charged" Tons	Recvd. Other Minerals Tons	Recvd. General Merchandise Tons	Coal & Coke "Not Charged" Tons	Total Goods Tonnage Tons	Coal & Coke "Not Charged" (excl.) Total Receipts £	Livestock (Fwd. & Recvd.) Wagons	Total Carted Tonnage Tons
Wrington (§)	1903	3	104	1,965	11,020	*	695	156	20	871	—	14	309	1,582	957	638	588	4,068	1,094	13	472
	1913	3	134	2,220	9,462	*	637	162	146	945	—	—	294	1,487	118	1,753	1,015	4,087	1,775	16	522
	1923	2	354	2,999	6,061	4	544	296	450	1,290	18	—	265	1,045	250	1,498	1,038	4,061	1,719	55	412
	1924	4	319	2,610	4,952	10	450	268	256	974	—	—	277	936	268	1,598	1,294	4,381	1,686	25	437
	1925	3	317	2,254	5,607	8	465	275	176	916	—	—	231	786	321	1,543	1,382	4,283	1,602	23	374
	1926	2	823	2,450	3,592	17	333	257	237	827	—	—	204	567	344	1,485	1,331	3,941	1,427	23	415
	1927	3	776	2,523	3,522	5	310	242	357	909	10	—	182	775	165	1,535	1,089	4,646	1,545	13	323
	1928	3	755	2,313	4,079	8	300	223	508	1,091	—	16	207	561	88	1,506	1,964	4,316	1,359	18	294
	1929	3	674	2,233	5,282	10	441	229	581	1,258	—	44	230	498	28	1,085	2,078	3,886	1,265	32	341
	1930	3	695	1,737	3,148	1	211	212	576	1,011	—	10	211	510	29	954	2,138	3,935	1,302	34	323
	1931	3	682	1,707	1,300	—	82	151	376	670	—	58	195	566	14	1,157	2,215	4,157	1,563	11	494
	1932	3	474	—	—	—	—	137	189	340	—	—	242	522	34	998	1,860	3,714	1,457	—	323
	1933	2	282	1,358	—	—	—	—	51	188	—	—	234	577	7	747	1,911	3,476	1,170	10	589
Langford (§)	1903	2	98	1,457	7,085	*	564	95	194	853	—	32	104	612	812	375	186	2,127	604	11	177
	1913	2	115	1,000	4,534	*	371	61	80	512	—	8	204	23	673	374	132	1,414	578	—	248
	1923	2	318	1,608	1,846	3	166	54	617	837	—	—	63	246	171	544	483	1,616	771	11	99
	1924	1	221	1,142	1,751	2	193	60	559	782	6	—	16	279	81	163	387	983	360	3	91
	1925	1	213	1,075	1,611	2	134	53	512	699	9	76	24	188	114	195	319	924	357	4	79
	1926	1	+	1,046	1,160	3	103	70	514	687	9	12	29	88	22	296	247	662	490	5	101
	1927	1	+	1,228	1,190	5	110	61	559	730	8	11	24	64	43	371	598	1,127	363	4	105
	1928	1	+	999	1,372	8	110	60	466	636	7	—	65	81	19	291	537	952	429	6	49
	1929	1	+	1,031	1,408	11	100	56	301	602	20	8	30	78	37	330	559	1,076	329	15	43
	1930	1	+	788	929	4	83	58	244	442	9	—	5	40	38	271	601	980	195	32	29
	1931	1	+	516	440	—	34	43	144	321	—	—	12	36	15	217	681	904	185	9	30
	1932	1	+	348	—	—	—	19	10	163	10	—	18	30	6	123	600	771	176	3	36
	1933	+	+	206	—	—	—	20	—	30	—	—	—	41	—	101	658	823	—	—	—
Burrington (§)	1913	1	87	1,576	4,860	5	448	173	455	1,076	—	7	103	386	185	838	760	2,270	500	—	211
	1923	1	219	1,533	2,106	2	244	101	312	657	—	2	200	—	708	466	778	2,149	876	1	127
	1924	1	224	1,545	1,913	—	207	88	436	731	—	20	74	88	825	399	589	1,900	814	2	117
	1925	1	211	1,454	2,049	—	211	118	508	827	—	—	161	43	438	355	651	1,648	627	—	108
	1926	1	+	1,277	1,635	—	188	106	504	794	—	15	50	188	164	301	575	1,303	480	1	95
	1927	1	+	1,296	1,789	—	200	111	423	797	—	—	104	192	191	341	592	1,463	561	2	102
	1928	1	+	1,248	1,588	—	144	130	343	617	—	—	88	102	208	388	547	1,320	631	1	78
	1929	1	+	1,241	1,499	—	202	132	349	688	—	—	46	102	222	388	547	1,170	558	1	70
	1930	1	+	1,149	1,122	—	150	128	293	571	10	—	70	298	74	370	615	1,397	578	2	56
	1931	1	+	803	456	—	56	82	94	232	10	—	106	234	248	230	600	1,421	571	1	61
	1932	+	+	655	—	—	—	21	54	75	—	34	45	151	449	141	684	1,008	580	1	42
	1933	+	+	275	—	—	—	20	1	21	—	—	—	94	44	—	—	—	254	—	104

* Not available. § Controlled by Congresbury from April, 1933. ‡ Included with Wrington.

TRAFFIC DEALT WITH AT STATIONS

Station	Year	Staff Supervisory and Wages (all Grades) No.	Paybill Expenses £	Total Receipts £	Tickets issued No.	Season Tickets No.	Passengers (including Season Tickets, etc.) £	Parcels £	Miscellaneous £	Total £	Fwd. Coal and Coke "Charged" Tons	Fwd. Other Minerals Tons	Fwd. General Merchandise Tons	Rec. Coal and Coke "Charged" Tons	Rec. Other Minerals Tons	Rec. General Merchandise Tons	Coal and Coke "Not Charged" (Fwd. & Rec.) Tons	Total Goods Tonnage Tons	Total Receipts £	Coal and Coke "Not Charged" (excluding) Tons	Livestock (Fwd. & Rec.) Wagons	Total Carted Tonnage Tons
Blagdon Branch (contd.).																						
Blagdon.. (§)	1903	3	180	1,876	9,419	*	598	84	229	879	—	—	207	668	690	1,032	91	2,800	907		11	252
	1913	3	209	1,961	6,469	*	598	46	764	1,396	—	—	405	1,942	53	125	23	2,528	565		8	158
	1923	4	532	1,496	3,407	4	465	117	191	773	—	—	92	1,437	41	172	14	1,776	723		16	139
	1924	1	277	1,118	2,702	6	408	146	160	674	—	—	42	721	27	138	16	780	444		4	114
	1925	1	196	1,148	3,087	7	386	163	93	642	—	35	51	480	159	151	304	956	506		14	129
	1926	1	+	886	2,225	5	307	57	59	423	—	50	25	—	143	620	—	1,108	463		7	84
	1927	1	+	1,203	2,356	9	259	58	91	438	—	—	25	1,504	44	151	8	1,883	765		11	105
	1928	1	+	1,019	1,673	2	190	44	64	298	—	—	19	2,226	19	125	7	2,411	721		17	50
	1929	Incl.		1,178				40	77	117	—	—	9	3,611	—	101	16	3,786	1,061		19	56
	1930	with		753				51	13	64	—	—	4	1,885	—	100	15	2,009	689		20	63
	1931	Wrington.		761				41	17	58	—	19	3	1,749	14	214	—	1,981	703		5	51
	1932			280				25		25	—	—	4	1,710	—	131	16	1,160	255		1	41
	1933			226				30		32	—	—		15	—	76	7	121	194		5	42
Total ..	1903	8	382	5,298	27,524	*	1,845	315	443	2,603	—	48	620	2,842	2,459	2,045	977	8,995	2,695		25	901
	1913	8	545	8,847	25,315	*	2,042	442	1,445	3,929	6	15	1,008	3,838	1,029	3,091	1,907	10,886	2,918		55	1,199
	1923	10	1,423	7,636	13,420	13	1,419	558	1,570	3,547	9	—	620	2,728	1,178	2,675	2,320	9,530	4,089		75	777
	1924	6	1,041	6,415	11,318	18	1,218	562	1,381	3,161	27	30	409	2,019	1,215	2,296	2,274	8,250	3,254		34	783
	1925	6	937	6,105	12,354	15	1,196	609	1,279	3,084	8	111	467	1,497	900	2,344	2,368	7,535	3,111		44	748
	1926	6	823	5,463	8,512	24	931	489	1,314	2,734	27	27	305	837	689	2,672	2,457	7,014	2,729		37	654
	1927	6	776	6,178	8,857	20	909	472	1,430	2,811	30	61	343	2,525	542	2,398	3,399	9,298	3,074		28	497
	1928	6	755	5,716	8,712	10	744	457	1,441	2,642	9	—	366	3,055	359	2,290	3,105	9,142	3,313		42	488
	1929	7	674	5,973	8,189	19	743	464	1,453	2,660	—	24	366	4,349	306	1,843	3,200	10,097	2,895		88	469
	1930	5	695	4,983	5,199	9	444	466	1,178	2,088	—	44	298	2,733	141	1,695	3,138	8,045	3,032		86	513
	1931	4	662	4,313	2,286	5	172	378	731	1,281	—	10	274	2,585	291	1,818	3,661	8,439	2,477		28	464
	1932	3	474	3,080				216	387	603	—	92	—	713	489	1,334	3,076	6,066			5	697
	1933	2	282	2,065				207	64	271	10	19	301	727	51	1,065	3,260	5,433	1,794		16	771

* Not available. † Controlled by Wrington. ‡ Included with Wrington. § Controlled by Congresbury from April, 1933.

WRINGTON VALE LIGHT RAILWAY

Single Line worked by Train Staff, and only one engine in steam at a time (or two or more coupled).

DOWN TRAINS. — WEEK DAYS ONLY.

Distance from C'gresbury		Mile Post Mileage		STATIONS.		Ruling Gradient 1 in	Goods	Goods RR
M.	C.	M.	C.				a.m.	a.m.
1	46	—	—	Yatton .... dep.		....	7 30	7 30	....
—	—	—	—	CONGRESBURY .. dep.		434 F.	7 46	7 46	..
2	72	2	64	Wrington..........	arr.	60 R.	7 56	7 56	....
					dep.	..		8 6
4	17	4	9	Langford	arr.	73 R.	....	8 12	....
					dep.	..	..	8 22	..
5	7	4	79	Burrington	arr.	50 R.	....	8 26	....
					dep.	..	..	8 40	..
6	49	6	41	BLAGDON	arr.	70 F.	....	8 50	....

UP TRAINS. — WEEK DAYS ONLY.

Distance from Blagdon		STATIONS.		Ruling Gradient 1 in	Goods	Goods RR	
M.	C.				a.m.	a.m.	
—	—	BLAGDON .... dep.		....	....	....	9 5	....
1	42	Burrington	arr.	70 R.	....	..	9 C15	..
			dep.	..	..		9 R20	....
1	65	Stop Board........ dep.		..	....		9 P22	..
2	32	Langford	arr.	50 F.	....	....	9 C26	..
			dep.	....	..		9 R31	..
3	57	Wrington..........	arr.	73 F.	..	..	9 38	....
			dep.	..	..	8 25	9 50	..
6	49	CONGRESBURY ..	arr.	60 F.	..	8 32	9 57	..
—	—	Congresbury ...... dep.		....	....	8 54	10 20	....
8	15	Yatton .... arr.		434 R.	..	9 0	10 26	..

The Engineers have absolute occupation of this Branch each morning from 5-0 a.m. until 15 minutes before the first train is due to leave Congresbury.

Time table, 26th September, 1938 to 2nd September, 1939.

Staff 1925		Staff 1926	
	£		£
Blagdon Class 5 station master	200	Blagdon Grade 1 porter	130
Burrington Class 5 station master	200	Burrington Grade 1 porter	130
Langford Class 5 station master	200	Langford Grade 1 porter	130
Wrington Class 5 station master	200	Wrington Class 4 station master	230
Wrington Grade 2 porter	120	Wrington junior clerk	55
		Wrington Grade 2 porter	120
			795
Yatton Grade 2 travelling			
porter assisting on branch	120		
	1,040		

A further economy was effected when the branch was temporarily closed from 9.00 am till 5.00 pm 5th to 7th October, 1925 for occupation by the Engineering Department. This resulted in a saving of £125 5s. 9d. over work which would otherwise have been carried out on Sundays at enhanced pay. On closure days, passengers were carried by road motor and goods trains run outside the hours of 9.00 am to 5.00 pm.

The branch received a further blow in 1926 when closure caused by the General Strike resulted in Messrs Nestlé using lorries for collecting churns from farms. In the post-strike era, all branch stations resumed handling milk traffic, but in reduced quantities. For example, Burrington's total of over 12,000 churns in 1913, was reduced by a half by 1930 and only 600 were carried in 1933.

The branch received a further review in 1928 and staff economies were recommended. At Blagdon the Grade 1 porter was to be withdrawn and an agent appointed to deal with parcels and goods traffic, the guard to issue tickets and stamp parcels received by agent - this was a small shop close to the station entrance. A more dramatic plan proposed, but not adopted, was closing the branch entirely and sending passengers and goods by road.

Due to light loading of passenger trains, these were declared uneconomic and the service ceased from 14th September, 1931 and, following the withdrawal of this service, milk was collected by GWR lorry. From the cessation of the passenger service, Burrington and Blagdon stations were unstaffed, the post of Wrington station master abolished and the Congresbury station master, W.G. Gait, given responsibility for the whole branch.

Another economy was that 'smalls traffic', i.e. items under one ton, for the Wrington branch were delivered by the Congresbury GWR lorry, though full wagon traffic still used the branch sidings. For several years the GWR had been developing its country lorry service in the Weston-super-Mare and Yatton areas. At some stations the carting agent was the local coal merchant, otherwise the delivery of 'smalls traffic' from branch stations was carried out by porters on foot, the Yatton lorry only used for heavier deliveries. The 'smalls' lorry, a rigid wheelbase Thornycroft No. 3224, registration number CLR 892, new in January 1936, was maintained at Weston-super-Mare and kept overnight in Congresbury goods shed. In winter its radiator was drained at night to prevent freezing and next morning filled with hot water obtained by the porter from the Wrington goods engine.

WRINGTON VALE LIGHT RAILWAY

Single Line worked by Train Staff, and only one engine in steam at a time (or two or more coupled).

PASSENGER SERVICE SUSPENDED.

DOWN TRAINS. WEEK DAYS ONLY.

Distance from C'gresbury.		Mile Post Mileage.		STATIONS.		Ruling Gradient 1 in		Frght. SX RR a.m.	
M.	C.	M.	C.						
1	46	—	—	Yatton .... dep.		....	....	....	....
—	—	—	—	CONGRESBURY .. dep.		434 F.	..	9 15	..
2	72	2	64	Wrington............ { arr.		60 R.	....	9 25	....
				dep.		..	..	9 35	
4	17	4	9	Langford .... { arr.		73 R.	....	9 41	....
				dep.		..	..	9 51	..
5	/7	4	79	Burrington ...... { arr.		50 R.	....	9 55	....
				dep.		..	..	10 10	..
6	49	6	41	BLAGDON .... arr.		70 F.	....	10 20	....

UP TRAINS. WEEK DAYS ONLY.

Distance from Blagdon		STATIONS.		Ruling Gradient 1 in			Frght. SX RR a.m.	
M.	C.							
—	—	BLAGDON .... dep.		....	....	....	10 30	....
1	42	Burrington ...... { arr.		70 R.	....	..	10 40	..
		dep.		..	..	....	10 50	....
1	65	Stop Board........ dep.		..	....	..	10 P52	..
2	32	Langford .... { arr.		50 F.	....	....	10 56	..
		dep.		....	....	..	11 1	..
3	57	Wrington.......... { arr.		73 F.	..	....	11 8	..
		dep.		..	..	..	11 18	..
6	49	CONGRESBURY .. arr.		60 F.	..	....	11 25	....
—	—	Congresbury ...... dep.		....	....	..	11 35	....
8	16	Yatton .... arr.		434 R.	..	....	11 41	..

The Engineers have absolute occupation of this Branch each morning from 5-0 a.m. until 15 minutes before the first train is due to leave Congresbury.

Time table, November 1950.

Branch Staff 1934

Congresbury	-	station master, 2 porters, 2 signalmen
Wrington	-	porter, who also worked level crossing gates
Langford	-	porter, who also worked level crossing gates
Burrington	-	nil
Blagdon	-	nil

Circa 1942 the Blagdon branch engine left Yatton shed and worked the 5.30 am mixed train to Clevedon and returned on the 6.35 to Yatton; then took the 6.55 am passenger to Wells and the 8.00 am return, arriving Yatton 8.39. The crew then had breakfast before taking the 9.10 am empty wagons from Yatton to Sandford Quarry and returning to Congresbury to work the Wrington branch, the wagons already having been left at Congresbury. The Congresbury porter travelled with the train to open the gates at Wrington and Langford crossings and also to collect wagon numbers at each station. A label was removed from one side of a wagon, recorded in the porter's book and these details later transferred to a book at Congresbury station. The date the wagons were emptied was also noted so that, if necessary, a demurrage charge could be made.

As the remaining traffic, chiefly coal, livestock and fertilisers to Langford, Burrington and Blagdon had become light, these stations were closed to freight on 1st November, 1950. The last timetable showed the weekdays-only freight leaving Congresbury at 9.15 am and arriving Blagdon 10.20. It left at 10.30 and arrived Congresbury 11.25 and Yatton 11.41.

The track was lifted by Thomas Ward, Sheffield, east of 3 miles 2 chains, work starting in January 1952 and being completed by April. Wrington continued to deal with full truck loads, principally coal, 'smalls' at this date being sent under the Zonal Delivery Scheme by road from Bristol. Although trains ran to Wrington on an 'as required' basis, in practice, a train ran daily Mondays to Fridays. Trains were allowed 10 minutes each way Congresbury to Wrington.

The last coal arrived at Wrington on Friday 7th June, 1963 and on the following day, although trains did not normally run on Saturdays, detonators exploded as the empties left the yard. The branch officially closed on 10th June, 1963 and on that very day BR erected a new sign at Iwood level crossing 'Beware of Trains'. Messrs Cohen lifted the track in May 1964. Following the line's closure, the yard at Wrington continued in use as a coal depot, fuel arriving by road. The Cheddar Valley line from Yatton to Cheddar through Congresbury closed entirely on 1st October, 1964, passenger trains having been withdrawn on 9th September, 1963.

BLAGDON BRANCH.					
Wrington Vale Line	Speed must not exceed at any point on the line in either direction ..	10
Brinsea Road Level Crossing		
Iwood Lane Level Crossing	Permanent Restriction of Speed Boards fixed	10
Copthorn Lane Level Crossing		
Bourne Lane Level Crossing		

Maximum speed of trains on the WVLR, 1945.

'58XX' class 0-4-2T No. 5809 with a down goods train, 31st August, 1950.   *D.W. Winkworth*

Guard Bert Maslen in his brake van, probably east of the River Yeo bridge west of Wrington.
Author's Collection

Maximum Speed of Trains through Junctions, etc.

NAME OF PLACE	DIRECTION OF TRAINS		Miles per Hour
	From	To	
CONGRESBURY AND WRINGTON			
Wrington Vale Line ... ...] Speed must not exceed at any point on [the line in either direction ... ...]			10
Brinsea Road Level Crossing ... ...} Permanent Restriction of Speed Boards fixed... ... ...]			10
Iwood Lane Level Crossing			

Maximum speed of trains on the WVLR, 9th June to 14th September, 1958.

Time table, 9th June to 14th September, 1958.

WEEKDAYS   WRINGTON VALE LIGHT RAILWAY

SINGLE LINE, worked by Train Staff and only one engine in steam at a time (or two or more coupled)

Mileage from Congresbury		Mile Post Mileage		DOWN	Ruling Gradient 1 in				Mileage		UP	Ruling Gradient 1 in		
M	C	M	C				SX Q am		M	C				SX Q am
1	46	—	—	Yatton..................... dep	—	.......|.......			—	—	Wrington .... dep	—	......|	11 25
									2	72	Congresbury ... ... arr	60 F	..	11 35
— 2	— 72	— 2	— 64	Congresbury	434 F	..|......	10 45				.... dep		......|	11 55
				Wrington .... arr	60 R	......		10 55	4	38	Yatton ... ... arr	434 R	..	12 1

The Engineers have absolute occupation of this Branch each morning from 5.0 a.m. until 15 minutes before the first train is due to leave Congresbury.

Ivatt class '2' 2-6-2T No. 41208 passes through Wrington station, 22nd October, 1962.   *Author*

No. 41208 returns from Sandford & Banwell with an ex-LMS brake van to pick up the Wrington goods train at Congresbury on 22nd October, 1962.   *Author*

The remains of Burrington station *c.*1963. The station house is prominent.   *Lens of Sutton*

Chapter Five

Locomotives

The branch, an 'uncoloured' route, enjoyed an interesting variety of motive power. The initial trains were worked by 2-4-0T No. 1384. This had been built by Sharp, Stewart & Co. as Works No. 2578 in February 1876 for the Watlington & Princes Risborough Railway where it became No. 2. When the GWR took over the Watlington company, it entered GWR stock in December 1883 and was renumbered 1384. Among other duties it was used on the construction of the Bodmin Road to Bodmin branch in 1886 and loaned to the Lambourn Valley Railway when it opened in April 1898.

In November 1899 No. 1384 was rebuilt at Swindon with a Belpaire boiler but the primitive cab, consisting of a bent sheet, was retained.

Dimensions of No. 1384 as rebuilt by the GWR in November 1899 were:

Wheelbase	5 ft 9 in. + 6 ft 8 in.
Leading wheels	2 ft 10½ in. diameter
Coupled wheels	4 ft 2 in. diameter
Belpaire boiler	134 x 1¾ in. tubes
Boiler pressure	120 lb. sq. in.
Heating surface	
Tubes	568.02 sq. ft
Firebox	52.89 sq. ft
Total heating surface	620.91 sq. ft
Grate area	8.77 sq. ft
Tank capacity	640 gallons
Weight	
Empty	19 tons 3 cwt
Full	24 tons 7 cwt

After a brief spell of only a few weeks on the WVLR it was used on the Culm Valley branch and withdrawn in April 1911, then sold to the Bute Works Supply Company. She was purchased by the Weston, Clevedon & Portishead Light Railway and worked on that line still bearing the GWR number plate 1384. In due course she was named *Hesperus*. She ended her career rather ignominiously on 5th April, 1934 when a wooden bridge at Wick St Lawrence collapsed under her weight.* No. 1384 was cut up in June 1937.

When No. 1384 left the WVLR, branch trains were generally worked by Armstrong's '517' class 0-4-2Ts, No. 518 being allocated to Blagdon in March 1914 and No. 837 in January 1921. In the 1920s 'Metro' class 2-4-0Ts appeared, though interestingly the only class of engine authorised in the 1st October, 1945 Working Time Table Appendix was the '517' class 0-4-2T with no mention made of either the 'Metro' class, or the '48XX'/'58XX' class 0-4-2Ts. The '517' class was limited to a load of 112 tons Congresbury to Blagdon and Blagdon to Burrington, but 280 tons over the easier road Burrington to Congresbury.

---

* For more details see *The Weston, Clevedon & Portishead Light Railway*, by Colin G. Maggs, The Oakwood Press (LP25).

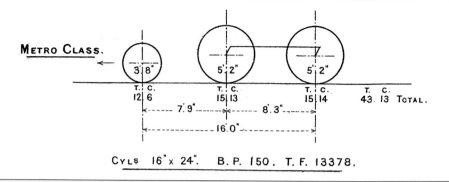

METRO CLASS.

3'8"   5'2"   5'2"

T. C.   T. C.   T. C.   T. C.
12 6   15 13   15 14   43.13 TOTAL.

7'9"   8'3"

16'0"

CYLS 16"x 24".   B. P. 150.   T. F. 13378.

Engine wheelbase diagrams showing dimensions and axle loads, 1902.

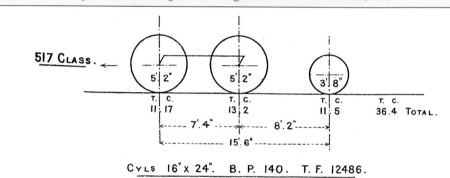

517 CLASS.

5'2"   5'2"   3'8"

T. C.   T. C.   T. C.   T. C.
11 17   13 2   11 5   36.4 TOTAL.

7'4"   8'2"

15'6"

CYLS 16"x 24".   B. P. 140.   T. F. 12486.

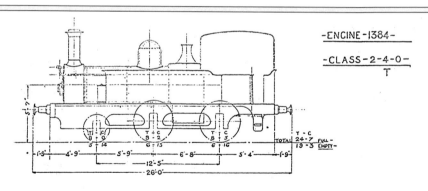

-ENGINE-1384-

-CLASS-2-4-0-
T

T C   T C
8 9   8 16
5 14 6 15

TOTAL 24·7 FULL
19·3 EMPTY

1'5"   4'9"   5'9"   6'8"   5'4"   1'9"

12'5"

26'0"

— DESCRIPTION —

CYLINDERS	DIAR 12" STROKE 17" STEAM PORTS 1" x 10" EXHAUST 2" x 10"
BOILER	BARREL 9'-0" DIAR OUTS 3'-2" & 3'-3½"
FIREBOX	OUTS 3'-2" x 3'-11" INS 2'-6¼ x 3'-3½ HEIGHT 4'-0½
TUBES	Nº 134 DIAR 1¾" LENGTH 9'-3½"
HEATING SURFACE	TUBES 568·02 SQ FT FIREBOX 52·89 SQ FT TOTAL 620·91 SQ FT
AREA OF FIREGRATE	8·77 SQ FT
WHEELS	LEADING 2'-10½" DRIVING 4'-2" TRAILING 4'-2"
WATER CAPACITY OF TANK	640 GALLONS
WORKING PRESSURE	150 LBS
TRACTIVE EFFORT	6610 LBS

Ex-GWR No. 1384 on the Weston, Clevedon & Portishead Light Railway at Portishead, 1911, in ex-GWR condition. The GWR number plate was retained until 1917 when the engine was named *Hesperus*. *Author's Collection*

MAXIMUM LOADS FOR BRANCH FREIGHT TRAINS

BRANCH.		WORKING LOADS. Maximum number of wagons to be conveyed except by Trains specially provided for in the Service Books or by arrangement.	MAXIMUM ENGINE LOADS. For engine groups see pp. 277 & 278.							
			For Group **A** Engines.				For Heavy Engines 2—8—0 "G" (R.O.D.)			
From	To		Class 1 Traffic.	Class 2 Traffic.	Class 3 Traffic.	Empties.	Class 1 Traffic.	Class 2 Traffic.	Class 3 Traffic.	Empties.
Wrington Vale.										
Congresbury ...	Blagdon... ...	20	6	7	9	12	Small Passenger Engine.			
Blagdon ...	Burrington ...	20	6	7	9	12				
Burrington ...	Congresbury ...	28	20	24	30	40				

Maximum loads. Appendix to Working Time Table 13th July-20th September, 1925.

Maximum loads, extract from the Working Time Table, 9th June to 14th September, 1958.

Maximum Loads for Branch Freight Trains

BRANCH		WORKING LOADS Maximum number of wagons to be conveyed except by Trains specially provided for in the Service Books or arrangement	MAXIMUM ENGINE LOADS																		
			For Group A Engines				For Group B Engines				For Group C Engines				For Group D Engines				For Group E Engines			
From	To		Class 1 Traffic	Class 2 Traffic	Class 3 Traffic	Empties	Class 1 Traffic	Class 2 Traffic	Class 3 Traffic	Empties	Class 1 Traffic	Class 2 Traffic	Class 3 Traffic	Empties	Class 1 Traffic	Class 2 Traffic	Class 3 Traffic	Empties	Class 1 Traffic	Class 2 Traffic	Class 3 Traffic	Empties
WRINGTON VALE																						
†Congresbury ... ...| Wrington...	20	6	7	9	12	...	...	...	...	...	...	...	...	...	...	...	...	...	...	...	...
†Wrington...	Congresbury ... ...| 28	20	24	30	40	...	...	...	...	...	...	...	...	...	...	...	...	...	...	...	...

†—14XX Class Engine. The instructions contained herein do not in any way affect or remove the prohibition placed by the Chief Engineer on the working of certain types of engines over certain sections of line although loadings may be given in the table for engines over portions of line which are prohibited for them.

In 1901, Joseph Loftus Wilkinson, General Manager of the GWR, sent the following letter to William Dean, dated before the appearance of Drummond's London & South Western Railway and London, Brighton & South Coast Railway Joint Committee's railcars which appeared in April 1903 and generally acknowledged as progenitors of the early 20th century steam rail motors:

(To William Dean)

23 October 1901

My Dear Sir

Wrington Vale Light Railway
As you know the Wrington Vale Light Railway will shortly be ready for opening.
We shall have to conduct the traffic for a time with ordinary stock.
I am desirous however, and the Chairman concurs, that we should try upon this Railway the experiment of working the passenger traffic by a Motor car, the idea being that the motor should be moved by Steam: be competent to run on the gradients between Yatton and Blagdon at a speed of 20 miles per hour, and to have accommodation for about 50 passengers (divided into two classes, say 10 First and 40 Second) ['Second' should read 'Third' - *author*].
The vehicle to be complete in itself and of course to be so designed that not more than 14 tons would be upon any one pair of wheels.
Yours faithfully,
J.L. Wilkinson

The correspondence continues:

(Dean to Wilkinson)

November 6 1901

My Dear Sir

Wrington Vale Light Railway
With reference to your letter of the 23rd ultimo and telegram of yesterday, I have since receipt of your letter been carefully considering the subject.
To the best of my recollection, the experiment of a combined engine and carriage was first tried upon the Eastern Counties Railway in 1847. Similar experiments have been tried in various forms on the Continent and in the United States of America.
I think it is reasonably likely that a design can be matured which would enable us to reduce the working expenses on such a line as the Wrington, and possibly on some other branch, on which the loads are light, but in my judgement, the balance of advantage would be in favour of having the motor constructed so as to be detachable from the carriage.
I remember that in the case of the City & South London, and the Liverpool Overhead Railways the Board of Trade raised objection to the motors being used for pushing as well as drawing, and I take it, therefore, that if a carriage and motor were combined upon on one frame, it would be necessary to provide either turntables, or triangles at both ends of the railway, so that the motor would always be in front.
Further, as to repairs, the carriage would not require to go into shop so frequently as the motor, and when in shop, the class of labour required on the carriage would be different from that which would be required for the motor.
Again, on the Wrington as well as on other branches, there will be a certain amount of coal and goods traffic to be dealt with besides shunting. This would be more advantageously done by a detachable motor.
I will wait your further communication before proceeding with a design.
Yours faithfully,
William Dean

(To William Dean)

8 November 1901

My Dear Sir

Wrington Vale Light Railway

I am much obliged for and am very interested by your letter of the 8th [*sic*] inst in which you are good enough to communicate some of the considerations which have presented themselves to your mind in thinking over the proposal that passenger traffic on the Wrington Vale Light Railway should be worked by a motor which would form an integral part of a passenger vehicle.

As will have been gathered from my conversation with Mr Churchward, the Wrington Vale is a line over which it may suit the Company to experiment in the direction of running a more frequent service than will ordinarily be followed in the case of Light Railways, although we recognize the fact that the number of passengers to be carried by each unit of the service may not be great; and with a view to the adoption of the most economical mode of working not only as regards running expenses, but also in respect of the maintenance of the permanent way and Staff and in other directions, authority will be asked for the employment of a motor instead of a steam locomotive, the idea being that such a motor and carriage on one frame could be so designed to work separately as a self-contained affair; or as an alternative that it could be designed in such a manner that it would admit of this being attached to and drawing other vehicles.

It was not contemplated that such a vehicle would be required to be turned at each end of the line; and I rather understood from Mr Churchward that it was practicable to avoid any necessity for doing this; but if as I now gather from your letter, considerations of repairs are sufficiently weighty to determine the matter, then the provision of a detached motor might have most to recommend it. This motor would I take it, run round its train at either end of the line in the ordinary manner, and it would working very much the same way as the ordinary branch line locomotive which has, of course, to run either funnel or bunker first as may be most convenient.

I am however quite content to wait to hear from you further, but it is right for me to say (as I did personally to Mr Churchward) that the subject has been discussed with the Chairman and some of the Directors, and we are all anxious to be the first in the field with what we determine to do.

Yours faithfully,

J.L. Wilkinson

In the event, Drummond's rail motor appeared before one built by the GWR, but the latter company did not drop the idea of using a new and more economic method of working light traffic on branch lines and a memo for the Chairman at the company's half-yearly meeting on 13th February, 1902 read:

Suggested Employment of Motor Cars on Branch Lines

The Great Western Railway Company are the owners of several branch lines of railway which excepting for their value as contributors of traffic to the Company's Main Lines, could not be regarded as remunerative owing to the cost of which is necessarily incurred in their maintenance and working.

The question of providing some cheaper method of working these branch lines, without reducing the efficiency of the train service, has for some time received the careful consideration of this Company with a view to the proposal being submitted for the approval of the Board of Trade.

The formation of a practicable proposal is not free from difficulties owing to the necessity for providing facilities not only for Passengers, but for Agricultural produce, Coal and Minerals, Live Stock and other traffic of a branch line which, whilst not a great volume, is of a fluctuating character and requires despatch.

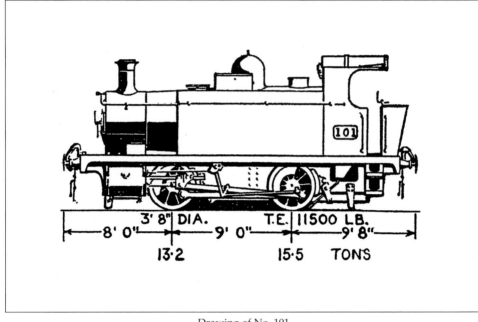

Drawing of No. 101

0-4-0T No. 101 specially designed for the WVLR but which never left Swindon.

Graham Bryant Collection

The matter is still under consideration, and the Company's Locomotive Superintendent is now engaged devising a motor car or light locomotive which would be suitable for employment in the circumstances indicated and would secure such economy as may be found practicable both in regards to the consumption of fuel and Stores and the employment of Staff. [At this February 1902 meeting the proprietors were asked to agree a vote of £12,000 for the Wrington Vale Light Railway, presumably for the construction of this locomotive.]

The correspondence continued:

(To Wilkinson)

18 March 1902

My Dear Sir
                              Wrington Vale Light Railway
   In reply to yours of 5th inst, we have the construction of a light locomotive for burning oil fuel well advanced and hope to have it ready for experimental running in the course of about three months.
   I will let you know as soon as it is ready for use.
                          Yours truly,
                          William Dean

(To Wilkinson)

29 May 1902

Dear Sir
               Oil Burning Locomotive for the Wrington Vale Light Railway
   In reply to yours of 17th inst, considerable further progress has been made since I wrote to you on the 18th March, and I think in about three weeks time you may be able to see the engine at work, experimentally in the yard at Swindon.
                          Yours truly,
                          William Dean

   The locomotive mentioned was No. 101 (i.e. a number in the experimental series) a chunky 0-4-0T, built in June 1902 but not taken into stock until a year later. It burnt oil fuel using James Holden's system (until 1885 when he left for the Great Eastern Railway, Holden had been Dean's chief assistant). It had outside Joy's valve gear modified to avoid the usual anchor link which would have been too near rail level. The unusual inner firebox opened out at the front to fit the tube area. The boiler barrel contained 289 1½ in. diameter tubes in its lower half, this large steam space compensating for the lack of an outer firebox. What appeared to be a Belpaire firebox casing was a short, square saddle tank for containing the oil fuel. Boiler pressure was a relatively high 180 lb. per square inch.
   The letters continued:

(To Wilkinson)

7 July 1902

Dear Sir
               Oil Burning Locomotive for the Wrington Vale Light Railway
   In reply to yours of 30th ultimo, unfortunately we have not yet been able to get this engine to work, but I will advise you as soon as we are in a position to let you know when it can be seen.
                          Yours truly,
                          G.J. Churchward*

---
* Churchward had succeeded Dean as Locomotive, Carriage & Wagon Superintendent on 1st June, 1902.

(To Wilkinson)

6 October 1902

Dear Sir

Oil Burning Locomotive for the Wrington Vale Light Railway

In reply to yours of 3rd instant, we have constructed this engine, but have found great difficulty in bringing the weight within the limit allowed on the Wrington Vale branch, and we are now putting another boiler on with the object, if possible, of improving the engine in this respect.

Yours truly,

G.J. Churchward

(To Churchward)

10 October 1902

Dear Sir

Oil Burning Locomotive for the Wrington Vale Light Railway

With reference to your letter of the 6th instant and our conversation on Wednesday last, I should be much obliged if you would arrange for the oil burning locomotive to be completed at the earliest possible date. I had not previously been made aware that the delay which has taken place had arisen from the difficulty of bringing the weight within the limit allowed on the Wrington Vale Light Railway [which] was selected as being a branch line upon which the conditions would be favourable to the experimental use of the Oil Motor, and, although I should like the Motor to work on the branch in question, this is not a *sine qua non*. if the difficulty you refer to has not been overcome it will be quite practicable for the trial to be made on the Salisbury, or some other suitable branch where the weight restriction does not obtain.

Yours faithfully,

J.L. Wilkinson

(To Churchward)

10 October 1902

Dear Sir

With reference to our conversation on Wednesday last, I have today written you in another letter upon the subject of the light oil locomotive which is under construction, but I desire in addition to say that from conversations I have had with Mr Dean and yourself, the impression has been left on my mind that what was under construction at Swindon was a vehicle combining a motor and carriage on one frame and which could be worked separately or with one or more trailing vehicles as described in Mr Dean's letter of the 6th November 1901.

The Chairman and Directors have been informed that it is in this direction that our experiments are being made, and having regard to the intiative in connection with the conveyance of traffic which is being manifested on all hands by other Railway Companies, it is essential that the Great Western Company should not be behind in designing some suitable means for working the omnibus traffic on their branch lines. I should therefore, be glad if you would give the question your special attention.

Yours faithfully,

J.L. Wilkinson

(To Wilkinson)

11 October 1902

Dear Sir

Oil Burning Locomotive for the Wrington Vale Light Railway

I will take no more notice of the weight question for the present, but will finish off the engine as quickly as possible.

The construction of a new boiler is involved, which will necessarily take some time.

Yours faithfully,

G.J. Churchward

Also on 11th October, 1902 Churchward wrote to Wilkinson that the total weight was not so great an object as keeping the weight down on individual axles: 'It may, therefore, be necessary to put a 6-wheeled bogie under one end of the car'. The proposed Wrington Vale rail motor became No. 1 on the Stroud Valley service, but the correspondence does not give a clue as to whether the mechanical parts were the same. Presumably the WVLR motor was given up because of the weight problem. A petrol driven rail car might have overcome the weight problem and is mentioned in a letter to Wilkinson:

21 April 1903

Dear Sir

I do not think the compartment system as shewn upon this print is so suitable as the ordinary tram car arrangement for this class of service, and tomorrow, or the next day at the latest, I shall be sending alternative designs embodying this.

The design of the petrol vehicle of which I spoke to you will also be ready tomorrow or the next day. In this case of course no coal or water have to be carried, but petrol only, but it is fair to say that up to the present no petrol driven vehicle of this kind has been successfully used. If it should be decided to make a trial it must be regarded as strictly experimental.

As to the steam driven vehicle, I do not think there is any doubt of its success from a mechanical point of view.

Yours faithfully,

G.J. Churchward

(It was decided not to proceed with a petrol-engined rail car and the GWR did not have one until 1911.)

In 1903 No. 101 was fitted with a Lentz boiler which consisted of a corrugated cylindrical firebox and a tapered boiler barrel. In the alterations the fuel saddle tank was removed and 200 gallons of oil stored in the rear ends of the side tanks. This modification was not successful and No. 101 was out of service from June 1904 until May 1905 when it emerged as a coal burner. The cab backplate was removed and a small bunker fitted. Due to its experimental nature, it was never used on the Wrington line and it was deemed wiser for it to spend its life shunting at Swindon works where it could receive proper care and attention. With a mileage of 36,458 it was condemned in September 1911.

Steam railmotors probably first ran over the Wrington branch on a date following 21st September, 1908 when they replaced the Clevedon three-coach set. The Clevedon branch railmotor ran to Wrington in the afternoon, while the Wrington branch locomotive and three-coach set worked the 2.52 pm Yatton to Clevedon and returned with the 3.40 pm mixed, making a further run to Clevedon at 4.05 pm and returning on the 4.32 pm.

Railmotors were unpopular with their crews as they tended to have either too much, or too little, steam and the footplate became very hot in summer. Water shortage could be a problem as there was no opportunity to replenish the 450 gallon tank between Yatton and Blagdon. Nevertheless, a report following a branch inspection on 11th November, 1925 said: 'The Clevedon motor takes curves and gradients without difficulty. Passenger traffic is light, but the economy of railmotors cannot be introduced because of loading, working and shunting restrictions on railmotors if the service was worked entirely by them'.

Steam railmotor No. 38 at Blagdon *c*.1926.   *M.E.J. Deane Collection*

'58XX' class No. 5809 on the Wrington branch *c*.1949: guard Bert Maslen, driver Sid Sledge and porter Colin Dyer.   *Author's Collection*

This problem was investigated and on 15th November, 1926 a modification to the Working Time Table read: 'The Sunday 7.8 am Yatton-Blagdon and 7.45 am Blagdon-Yatton worked by No. 4 Rail Motor Car. A Rail Motor may be allowed to enter sidings at Blagdon providing the speed does not exceed a walking pace when doing so'. It would appear that someone interpreted this to mean 'Shunt with a rail motor' as the September 1931 time table stated: 'No vehicle other than a trailer must be attached to any rail motor car working over this Branch. Rail Motor Cars are prohibited from going into the Sidings, or shunting, on the Branch'.

In freight-only days, trains were hauled by light axle loading engines such as 'Dean Goods' 0-6-0s. The only tank engines permitted were 0-4-2Ts of the '14XX' (auto-fitted) and '58XX' (non-auto) classes. The '58XX' engine kept at Yatton was primarily for the Wrington goods and if used on the Clevedon branch passenger trains had to be run round at each terminus - a tiring procedure, though one driver on these occasions, left the controls to the fireman on the Clevedon to Yatton trip and stood in the driving compartment of the auto coach giving the appearance of driving. Another ruse adopted when using a non-auto fitted engine on the Clevedon line was to run-round during daylight hours when an official was more likely to spot the offence, but after dark leave the engine at the Clevedon end.

On at least one occasion an 0-4-2T came off the road at Blagdon. The driver believed a point lever had been pulled right over and proceeded along the line, but due to freezing frost on the rodding, the points were still open. At a good speed the engine came off the road and was up to its axles in mud. Porter Malcolm Wathen borrowed a cycle from a girl engaged on sack repair and rode to Congresbury with the staff to give the breakdown train authority to enter the branch.

When the Western Region was allocated ex-LMS and BR class '2' locomotives of the 2-6-0 and 2-6-2T wheel arrangement, they were authorised to operate over the branch as long as they did not exceed the 14 ton maximum axle load. The first recorded visit of an Ivatt 2-6-0 was on 12th April, 1955, while the eight-coach Railway Correspondence & Travel Society's special to Wrington on 28th April, 1957 was hauled by Ivatt class '2' 2-6-2Ts Nos. 41202 and 41203.

The Locomotive Shed

Several authors have written that a single road, timber-built shed at Blagdon burned down in October 1912, but no photographic or other evidence of a locomotive shed there has come to light and the present author believes that one never existed, a tarpaulin merely being thrown over the engine at night.

The locomotive staff at Blagdon comprised a driver and two firemen, one of whom was passed for driving duty. One fireman started early and lit up, while his colleague on late turn dropped the engine's fire in the evening. At one time the regular driver had the delightful name of Oliver Oliver, colloquially known as 'Oliver Twice'. The locomotive department used a grounded coach body as a mess room. The branch engine pumped water from a well at Blagdon, steam

The Railway Correspondence & Travel Society's special 'The North Somerset Rail Tour' at Wrington on 28th April, 1957 at Wrington. Ivatt class '2' 2-6-2T No. 41202 runs round the train with No. 41203 to follow shortly. Bert Hurst, the RCTS Tours Organiser is on the left. Notice the trap point towards the lower right-hand corner.   *Author's Collection*

Yatton locomotive shed *c*.1955 with the breeze block locomen's cabin in the centre. An 0-4-2T stands outside the shed while a 2-6-2T moves an ash wagon. The gas tank wagon for recharging the Clevedon branch auto trailers can be seen.   *M.E.J. Deane*

for this purpose coming from the whistle. The water was for locomotive and lavatory use.

On 31st March, 1924 the branch locomotive changed its stabling point from Blagdon to Yatton and the branch time table was revised in order that the engine could start and end the day at Yatton instead of Blagdon. This transfer saved the locomotive department an engine and one set of men.

The single road, stone-built shed at Yatton, was a sub-shed to St Philip's Marsh (GWR code 32, SPM) until 1st January, 1941 when it became a sub-shed of Bath Road (22, BRD). From 1930 to 1952 Yatton (GWR code 182) had six drivers, six firemen, two shedmen, one chargeman cleaner and a cleaner, together with one shedman on night shift and the other on the day turn. The cleaner on nights started at 10.00 pm emptying the smokebox and ashpan of the Wrington engine. In the 1920s the shed had two regular engines plus a steam railmotor. In later days, the shed stud consisted of a '45XX' class 2-6-2T, an auto-fitted 0-4-2T and a non-fitted 0-4-2T.

Ivatt class '2' 2-6-2T No. 41202 and '14XX' class 0-4-2T No. 1454 at Yatton on 1st December, 1957.   *D. Fleming*

2-4-0T No. 1384 and Wrington Vale Light Railway branch passenger set at Rushey Platt Junction, Swindon, Autumn 1901. Note that the coaches have two running boards to cope with both standard and non-standard platform heights.

Author's Collection

Chapter Six

The Passenger Train Services

Passenger trains normally consisted of a 3-coach 4-wheel set, strengthened at times of heavy traffic. This set, composed of two brake thirds each weighing 11 tons 2 cwts flanking a composite of 10 tons 13 cwt, accommodated 20 first class and 36 third class passengers. The set, one of the last 4-wheelers to be built by the GWR, was in use throughout the lifetime of the branch passenger service and the WVLR was one of the few lines where the GWR was still using 4-wheeled coaches in the 1930s. The set was gas lit and equipped with low-level alighting boards to assist passengers at the low height branch platforms. When the set was undergoing repair, a single bogie brake composite was utilised.

When the train service opened on 11th December, 1901 four trains ran each way daily on weekdays, one being 'mixed', though at times when goods traffic was in excess of the maximum load of the mixed train, a separate goods train was run. A scheduled goods train worked from Blagdon to Wrington and back over the most steeply graded section of the branch. Down passenger trains were scheduled to take 26 minutes from Congresbury to Blagdon; up trains 23 minutes, while mixed trains were allowed 37 and 35 minutes respectively. Speed was restricted to an overall 25 mph and 10 mph at ungated level crossings. Principal destinations of passengers were Bristol and Weston-super-Mare.

By October 1903 the train service had been increased to five each way, the first up and down train using Congresbury and not Yatton as a starting or terminal station. By July 1914 the five trains each way were augmented in July and August by a 7.35 pm ex-Blagdon and 8.30 pm from Yatton, but this was withdrawn the following summer as a wartime economy measure. There was also an evening service each way on Sundays. In 1919 the passenger service was reduced to three each way, but the fourth was reintroduced on 3rd October, 1921 using the Clevedon branch railmotor which left Yatton at 12.57 pm and Blagdon 1.32 pm. An early Sunday morning service was begun in January 1925 to collect milk churns. In an attempt to regain traffic from buses, in 1926 a 7.20 am from Yatton was introduced, returning at 7.38 am from Wrington (it did not run through to Blagdon). It was insufficiently patronised so was withdrawn from 4th July, 1927, leaving the passenger service with four trains each weekday and one on Sundays. When Blagdon engine 'shed' closed on 31st March, 1924, the passenger service was re-cast so that the first train of the day started from Yatton and not Blagdon. In September 1930 the passenger service was reduced to two trains daily (morning and evening) and the Sunday service was withdrawn. The passenger service ceased on 14th September, 1931.

Day trips had been offered from Bristol stations to Burrington (for the Combe), and Blagdon (for the lake), while another attraction was to travel to Langford by rail and then by charabanc over the Mendips Hills to Cheddar whence the return to Bristol was made by rail. This trip was also offered in the reverse direction. On 7th July, 1903 about 70 members of the Bristol Master Builders' Association availed themselves of this facility. At Temple Meads they took reserved seats in

WRINGTON VALE LIGHT RAILWAY.

Single Line, worked by Train Staff, and only one Engine in Steam at a time (or two or more coupled).

UP TRAINS.	WEEK DAYS.				
		1	**2**	**3**	**4**	**5**
STATIONS.		A	A	D	A	A
		Pass.	Pass.	Goods	Pass.	Mixed

M	C	STATIONS		A.M.	A.M.	P.M.	P.M.	P.M.
—	—	Blagdon ...	dep.	8 0	9 35	1 0	2 35	5 20
1	37	Burrington ...	dep.	8 5	9 40	—	2 40	5 25
—	—	Stop Board ...	dep.	—	—	1 P 4	—	—
2	29	Langford {	arr.	8 8	9 43	1 8	2 43	5 30
			dep.	8 9	9 44	1 18	2 44	5 33
3	52	Wrington {	arr.	8 14	9 49	1 25	2 49	5 40
			dep.	8 15	9 50	—	2 50	5 45
6	31	Congresbury	arr.	8 23	9 58	....	2 58	5 55
—	—	Congresbury	dep.	8 26	10 1	..	3 1	6 2
7	75	Yatton ...	arr.	8 30	10 5	....	3 5	6 7

DOWN TRAINS	WEEK DAYS.				
		1	**2**	**3**	**4**	**5**
STATIONS.		A	A	D	A	A
		Pass.	Mixed	Goods.	Pass.	Pass.

M	C	STATIONS		A.M.	A.M.	P M.	P.M.	P.M.
		Yatton ..	dep.	8 40	11 ‖ 0	....	3 50	6 50
		Congresbury	arr.	8 43	11 ‖ 3	..	3 53	6 53
—		Congresbury	dep.	8 44	12 Q 3	....	3 54	6 54
2	59	Wrington {	arr.	8 52	12 11	..	4 2	7 2
			dep.	8 53	12 16	1 40	4 3	7 3
4	2	Langford {	arr.	8 59	12 23	1 48	4 9	7 9
			dep.	9 0	12 28	2 0	4 10	7 10
4	74	Burrington ..	dep.	9 6	12 35	—	4 16	7 16
6	31	Blagdon	arr.	9 10	12 40	2 8	4 20	7 20

Q Coaches for this Train will leave Yatton at rear of 11.50 a.m. Passenger.

Time table, January 1902.

An unidentified 0-4-2T and the three-coach branch set stand at Blagdon *c.*1908. On the left is an old tender, painted white, for the locomotive's water supply, it was fitted with a pump. Just to the right of it is the grounded coach body. The engine was kept overnight in the siding on the far left with a tarpaulin thrown over it. The station building has been extended towards the camera. On the far right is a shop near the entrance to the station drive.   *Author's Collection*

An up passenger train approaches Wrington *c.*1910. Notice between the lamp standard and churns is the ladder for lighting the lamps. The white post, right, marks the change in gradient from 1 in 427 down to 1 in 295 up.   *Author's Collection*

WRINGTON VALE LIGHT RAILWAY.

Single Line, worked by Train Staff, and only one Engine in Steam at a time (or two or more coupled).

Distance from Congresbury.		DOWN TRAINS. STATIONS.	Station Number.	WEEK DAYS							SUN-DAYS
				1	2	3	4	5	6	7	1
				B	B	K	B	B	B	B	B
				Pass.	Pass.	Goods.	Pass.	Pass.	Pass.	Pass. W	Pass.
M	C			A.M.	A.M.	P.M.	P.M.	P.M.	P.M.	P.M.	P.M.
1	46	Yatton .. dep.	1131	....	10 15	...	2 15	4 2	6 45	8 30	7 25
—	—	Congresb'ry dep	1217	8 19	10 19	12 10	2 19	4 6	6 49	8 34	—
2	72	Wrington { arr.	1210	—	—	12 20	—	—	—	—	7 36
		{ dep.		8 28	10 28	12 30	2 28	4 15	6 58	8 43	7 37
4	17	Langford { arr.	1211	—	—	12 36	—	—	—	—	—
		{ dep.		8 35	10 35	12 45	2 35	4 22	7 5	8 50	—
5	7	Burring- { arr.	1212	—	—	12 50	—	—	—	—	7 48
		ton { dep.		8 41	10 41	12 55	2 41	4 28	7 11	8 56	7 49
6	49	Blagdon .. arr.	1215	8 45	10 45	1 0	2 45	4 32	7 15	9 0	7 53

Distance from Blagdon.		UP TRAINS. STATIONS.	WEEK DAYS.							SUN-DAYS
			1	2	3	4	5	6	7	1
			B	B	K	B	B	B	B	B
			Pass.	Pass.	G'ds	Pass.	Pass.	Mixd	Pass. W	Pass.
M.	C.		A.M.	A.M.	A.M.	P.M.	P.M.	P.M.	P.M.	P.M.
—	—	Blagdon dep.	7 25	9 23	10 55	1 25	3 5	5 25	7 35	6 10
1	42	Burrington { arr.	—	—	11 0	—	—	—	—	—
		{ dep.	7 29	9 28	11 5	1 30	3 10	5 30	7 40	6 15
1	65	Stop Board dep.	—	—	11P 7	—	—	—	—	—
2	32	Langford { arr.	—	—	11 11	—	—	5 33	—	—
		{ dep.	7 33	9 32	11 21	1 34	3 14	5 36	7 44	—
3	57	Wrington { arr.	—	—	11 28	—	—	5 42	—	6 23
		{ dep.	7 39	9 38	11 40	1 40	3 20	5 47	7 50	6 26
6	49	Congresbury arr.	7 48	9 46	11 48	1 48	3 28	5 55	7 58	—
—	—	Congresbury dep.	....	9 48	....	1 51	3 31	6 2	8 0	—
8	15	Yatton arr.	..	9 52	..	1 55	3 35	6 7	8 5	6 38

W Runs during July and August only.

The Engineers have absolute occupation of this Branch each morning from 5 a.m. until 15 min. before the first train is due to leave Blagdon.

Time table, July 1914.

BLAGDON.

	a.m.	p.m.	a.m.				h. m.	
Jones .. .. Branch Guard No. 108.	8 25	4 25	. 8 40 11 30	Blagdon .. Blagdon ..	.. ..	Congresbury and back. Congresbury and back.	 8 0	
Porter Guard No. 109.			p.m. 5 0	Blagdon ..	..	Congresbury and back.	 8 0	

Programme of working of passenger guards and rail motor car conductors, 1st February, 1919.

Steam railmotor No. 38 at Blagdon c.1926. This motor was built in March 1905, withdrawn in December 1927 and converted to auto trailer No. 146, finally being condemned in August 1953.
M.E.J. Deane Collection

Guard Bert Maslen (*left*) and porter Sam Bragg (*right*) handling empty 17 gallon milk churns at
Yatton into the Wrington Vale branch train.   *Author's Collection*

WRINGTON VALE LIGHT RAILWAY

Single Line, worked by Train Staff, and only one Engine in Steam at a time (or two or more coupled).

Distance from Congresbury		DOWN TRAINS. STATIONS.	Station Number.	Ruling Gradient 1 in.	WEEK DAYS					SUN-DAYS
					1 Pass.	2 Pass.	3 Goods.	4 Motor.	5 Pass.	1 Pass.
M.	C.				A.M.	A.M.	P.M.	P.M.	P.M.	A.M.
1	46	Yatton .. dep.	1131		8 15	10 15	..	3 10	6 45	7 8
—	—	Congresb'ry dep	1217	434 F	8 19	10 19	12 35	3 14	6 49	7 13
2	72	Wrington { arr.	1210	60 R	—	—	12 45	—	—	—
		dep.			8 28	10 28	12 55	3 23	6 58	7 23
4	17	Langford { arr.	1211	73 R	—	—	1 1	—	—	—
		dep.		....	8 35	10 35	1 10	3 30	7 5	7 30
5	7	Burring- { arr.	1212	50 R	—	—	1 14	—	—	—
		ton { dep.		....	8 41	10 41	1 20	3 36	7 11	7 35
6	49	Blagdon .. arr.	1215	70 F	8 45	10 45	1 25	3 40	7 15	7 38

Distance from Blagdon.		UP TRAINS. STATIONS.	Ruling Gradient 1 in.	WEEK DAYS.					SUN-DAYS
				1 Pass.	2 Goods.	3 Pass.	4 Motor.	5 Pass.	1 Pass. and milk.
M.	C.			A.M.	A.M.	P.M.	P.M.	P.M.	A.M.
—	—	Blagdon dep.	..	8 55	11 20	1 35	3 45	7 25	7 45
1	42	Burrington { arr.	70 R	—	11 25	—	—	—	—
		{ dep.	..	9 2	11 34	1 40	3 50	7 30	7 52
1	65	Stop Board dep.	....	—	11 36	—	—	—	—
2	32	Langford { arr.	50 F	—	11 40	—	—	—	7 55
		{ dep.	.	9 6	11 48	1 44	3 54	7 34	7 59
3	57	Wrington { arr.	73 F	—	11 55	—	—	—	8 6
		{ dep.	..	9 12	12 10	1 51	4 1	7 41	8 8
6	49	Congresbury arr.	60 F.	9 20	12 18	1 59	4 9	7 49	8 16
—	—	Congresbury dep.		9 23	....	2 1	4 11	7 51	8 20
8	15	Yatton arr.	434 R	9 28	..	2 5	4 15	7 55	8 24

No vehicle other than the trailer must be attached to any rail motor car working over this Branch. Rail Motor Cars are prohibited from going into the Sidings, or shunting, on the Branch.

The Engineers have absolute occupation of this Branch each morning from 5 a.m. until 15 min. before the first train is due to leave Blagdon.

Time table, 13th July to 20th September, 1925.

Right: A Langford-Wrington ticket, fare 1½d. It is numbered 7480, so the traffic between these stations was quite brisk.   *Author's Collection*

Below: Yatton to Blagdon, third class ticket.

Right: Luggage label.

Below: '517' class 0-4-2T No. 540 at Blagdon on 22nd May, 1929 with the 7.20 pm to Yatton.   *H.C. Casserley*

WRINGTON VALE LIGHT RAILWAY

Single Line, worked by Train Staff, and only one Engine in Steam
at a time (or two or more coupled).

Distance from Congresbury		DOWN TRAINS. STATIONS.	Station Number.	Ruling Gradient 1 in.	WEEK DAYS ONLY.					
					Pass.	Goods.		Pass.		
M	C				A.M.	A.M.		P.M.		
1	46	Yatton .. dep.	1131	..	8 15	10 5	..	6 40	..	..
—	—	Congresb'ry dep	1217	434 F	8 19	10 30	...	6 44	....	....
2	72	Wrington { arr. dep.	1210	60 R	.. / 8 28	10 40 / 10 50	.. /	— / 6 53	.. / ..	.. / ..
4	17	Langford { arr. dep.	1211	73 R	.. / 8 35	10 56 / 11 5	.. / ...	— / 7 0	.. / ...	.. / ....
5	7	Burring-ton { arr. dep.	1212	50 R	.. / 8 41	11 9 / 11 15	.. /	11 / 7 6	.. /	.. / ....
6	49	Blagdon .. arr.	1215	70 F	.. 8 45	11 25	..	7 10	..	..

Distance from Blagdon.		UP TRAINS. STATIONS.	Ruling Gradient 1 in.	WEEK DAYS ONLY.					
				Pass.	Goods.		Pass.		
M	C			A.M.	A.M.		P.M.		
—	—	Blagdon dep.	..	8 55	11 50		7 20	..	..
1	42	Burring-ton { arr. dep.	70 R	— / 9 2	12 15 / 12 20	CR Stop Water Works Siding 15 mins. allowed.	— / 7 25	...	....
1	65	Stop Board dep.	....	—	12P22		—	..	..
2	32	Langford { arr. dep.	50 F	— / 9 6	12 26 / 12 31		— / 7 29	..	..
3	57	Wrington { arr. dep.	73 F	— / 9 12	12 38 / 12 48		— / 7 36	..	..
6	49	Congresb'ry arr	60 F	9 20	12 56		7 44	..	..
—	—	Congresb'ry dep	....	9 23	1 5		7 46	..	..
8	15	Yatton arr.	434 R	9 28	1 11		7 50	....	..

No vehicle other than the trailer must be attached to any rail motor
car working over this Branch. Rail Motor Cars are prohibited from
going into the Sidings, or shunting, on the Branch.

The Engineers have absolute occupation of this Branch each morning
from 5 a.m. until 15 min. before the first train is due to leave Blagdon.

Time table, September 1931. The last passenger time table.

the 10.30 am Cheddar Valley train. Their coaches were detached at Yatton and conveyed as a special to Langford. Here the party transferred to horse-drawn brakes. They visited Burrington Combe and lunched at Cheddar, going on to Wells for tea. They returned via the Cheddar Valley line. Although 1903 had unfavourable weather, that year approximately 5,500 passengers availed themselves of the Burrington Combe and Cheddar Gorge trip.

The funeral of Colonel Evan Llewellyn, Director of the GWR from 1898 and also of Bristol Waterworks and protagonist of the WVLR, took place at Burrington on 3rd March, 1914 involving interesting train working. He had died at Topsham on 27th February. The cause was heart failure following a bronchial attack. His body left there at 11.09 am in a brake composite and at Exeter, St David's this was transferred to the 11.02 am from Paignton which made a special stop at Yatton.

A special consisting of two brake composites and a Directors' saloon, left Temple Meads at 1.50 pm, at Yatton picked up the coach containing the deceased and departed from Yatton at 2.15 pm for Blagdon. This 2.15 to Blagdon comprised the branch engine, the Bristol engine, two Bristol coaches, the Directors' saloon, the coach containing the coffin and bringing up the rear was the three-coach branch set.

As a service train, it called at all stations with the branch coaches at the platform, but at Burrington halted with the special coaches at the platform and then drew forward for branch passengers.

Banks bordering the stations were tastefully laid out and 'blazed with primrose bloom'. Llewellyn's coffin was placed on a 4-horse farm wagon 'beautifully adorned with blooms'. The funeral was held in Burrington church where today he is commemorated on a brass plaque inside the church on the south wall near the side chapel, while outside his grave and cross-shaped tombstone may be seen near the foot of the tower's west wall.

On the train's arrival at Blagdon, the special coaches were shunted off and the two engines worked the branch set on the regular 3.05 pm Blagdon to Yatton. (Two engines had to be used because of the regulation 'One engine in steam or two coupled together'). At Congresbury the Bristol engine was sent back light to Blagdon to work the 3.55 pm return special to Temple Meads.

Colonel Evan Llewellyn's gravestone in Burrington churchyard, 14th July, 2003. *Author*

The Railway Correspondence & Travel Society's special 'The North Somerset Rail Tour' approaches Wrington on 28th April, 1957 with the guard coming forward to open the gates. The train left Waterloo behind No. 30453 *King Arthur* which drew it to Reading. Later No. 3440 *City of Truro* took it over the Bristol & North Somerset Railway and the train was hauled from the Bristol area by Ivatt class '2' 2-6-2Ts No. 41202 (lined) and No. 41203 (unlined).

Hugh Ballantyne

The two engines haul the special into Wrington. Notice part of the Wrington station's roof guttering is missing. *Grahame Farr*

Wrington on 28th April, 1957. The importance and intricacies of operating the special evidently prompted the presence of the district inspector in uniform.   *Author's Collection*

The RCTS special at Wrington with All Saints' church in the background.   *M.E.J. Deane*

No. 41202 lays over in the loop at Wrington. Because the train was too long for the loop, intricate shunting movements were required to enable the two locomotives to run-round the train.

Michael Farr

The train returning from Wrington.

R.J. Leonard, courtesy Colin Roberts

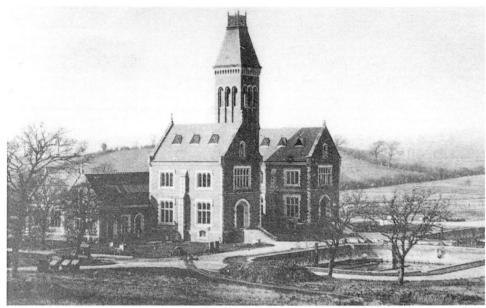

The Bristol Waterworks pumping station at Blagdon *c.*1910. The sidings entered the transept, left, and the corresponding one on the right. The tower contains the chimney. The receiving tank is in the foreground. *Author's Collection*

Blagdon pumping station on 6th August, 2000, view west. The chimney has been shortened following the installation of electric pumps. *Author*

Chapter Seven

Blagdon Reservoir and Pumping Station

In 1888 Parliament gave approval for the construction of the Yeo Reservoir. Work began in 1891, the reservoir started to fill in 1899 and first reached the top level in 1903. When full it contains 1,860 million gallons and supplies 2,100 million gallons per annum. The reservoir is 1.65 miles long; the perimeter of the water's edge is 7.2 miles; maximum depth is 42 ft and the average depth 14 ft. The 47 ft-high, 700 yd-long earth dam, 300 ft-wide at its base, extends 175 ft down into solid rock. Pethick Brothers, of Plymouth, who built the reservoir, had the construction of the Vale of Rheidol Railway as their next contract and used much of the equipment from Blagdon.

Until April 1949, four compound beam engines were used for pumping. They were built and erected between 1902 and 1905 by Glenfield & Kennedy of Kilmarnock. The three beam engines were capable of pumping a total of 7.5 million gallons daily, the fourth engine either being serviced or on standby. Each engine had a high pressure and low pressure cylinder connected to a 34 ft-long beam. Linked to each beam was a bucket pump with an output of 107 gallons per stroke to a head of 235 ft.

Steam was supplied by four boilers with two more held on standby. With two engines running, coal consumption was 8½ tons per day, making a total of about 3,100 tons per year. When two steam pumps were in use the total labour required was nine:

Engine room:	1 engine driver on each of 3 shifts + 1 day man
Boiler room:	1 stoker on each of 3 shifts
Two coal trimmers:	1 for each of two shifts 6.00am-10.00 pm

The four railway sidings were laid directly into the coal house.

On 8th May, 1902 C. Hawkesley, who superintended the building of the pumping station and was that year's president of the Institution of Civil Engineers, brought about 150 members and 50 other guests including Bristol Waterworks and GWR officials, to Blagdon for an inspection of the works. They arrived at Blagdon in a special train.

In 1949 the two beam engines in the north wing were replaced by two electric pumps, one capable of pumping 4 million gallons daily, the other 2 million gallons. The two remaining beam engines in the south wing were preserved as a museum feature. Today the electric pumping station operates remotely and can be controlled from the head office at Bristol. The pump house chimney was originally 130 ft high, but following electrification, in 1954 the upper 50 ft was removed.

The reservoir opened for public angling on 21st May, 1904. Fishing was excellent, the heaviest brown trout caught that year weighing 9 lb. 2 oz., while in 1910 a massive one of 16 lb. 4 oz. was landed.

The following standard gauge locomotives were used on the Blagdon Reservoir construction contract:

Inside cylinder 0-6-0ST Manning, Wardle, Works No. 21 of 1861, which after completion of the Blagdon contract became Hundred of Manhood & Selsey Tramway No. 2 *Sidlesham*.

Outside cylinder 0-4-0ST Beyer, Peacock, Works No. 1736 of 1877, and after the Blagdon contract was sold to Farrington Collieries Co.

Bristol Waterworks used a 600 mm gauge tramway for maintaining the reservoir. The engine was a Baguley Cars Ltd 0-4-0 petrol-mechanical, Works No. 736 of 1918, purchased from the War Department in September 1921. After being out of service for many years, it was sold in June 1971.

BLAGDON.
Water Works and Wills's Sidings.

The Points at these Sidings (both of which are situated about ¼-mile from Blagdon Station) will be worked with Annett's Key attached to the Train Staff. Traffic for the Sidings must be worked to Blagdon Station, and specially from Blagdon when necessary; and traffic from the Sidings must be worked to Blagdon Station. The Station Master at Blagdon must accompany the Special to these Sidings, and work the Ground Frame.

Traffic for and from these Sidings may be worked from and to Blagdon Station without brake-van. Trucks must be always drawn from Blagdon to the Sidings, and pushed from the Sidings to Blagdon, the Guard riding in the last truck from Blagdon, and in the leading truck from the Sidings, with the usual hand signals. Two sprags and two scotches must be kept at the Junction with the Sidings. Traffic to or from the Sidings must not be worked after dark.

Appendix to the Service Time Table, March 1910: instruction for working Water Works and Wills's Sidings.

Appendix

Railways Associated with the WVLR Proposed in the 20th Century

The Blagdon & Pensford Light Railway

On 29th November, 1904 the GWR's General Manager J.C. Inglis wrote a letter saying that Lord Waldegrave wished to induce the GWR to extend its Wrington line from Blagdon to Hallatrow, through property over which he owned the mineral rights: coal, stone suitable for agricultural lime, and iron ore 'which will become marketable as the supply of Spanish ores approach exhaustion'.

The amount of coal in the parishes was impressive:

Chewton Mendip	50,383,200 tons
Litton	31,752,320 tons
Hinton Bluett	63,985,380 tons
East Harptree	24,424,640 tons
West Harptree	42,909,370 tons
Compton Martin	84,215,000 tons
Ubley	18,906,000 tons

The GWR questioned whether Blagdon-Hallatrow was preferable to Blagdon-Pensford and observed that the coal measures would be below either route.

Following the granting of a Light Railway Order for the WVLR, villages further up the valley also desired rail communication. Although looking on favourably, the GWR was unwilling to finance such an undertaking, anticipating it to be of social, rather than economic benefit, so left it to local people to obtain an Order.

A meeting under the chairmanship of Sir Edward Strachey of Sutton Court, Bishop Sutton, was held in the Grand Hotel, Bristol on 5th January, 1905. Strachey, promoting the Blagdon & Pensfold Light Railway, promised to take payment in railway shares for his land that was required and, in addition, subscribe heavily. W. Foxlee, a member of the Institution of Civil Engineers, said that:

. . . the proposed railway which would be about 10¼ miles in length, commenced by a junction with the existing Wrington Vale Light Railway at Blagdon, and proceeded along the southern side of the Bristol Waterworks' Reservoir. Passing Ubley and a little to the north of Compton Martin, it crossed the main road from the Harptrees near the Blue Bowl Inn; thence, turning in a north-easterly direction, it followed the main road to Sutton Wick for a distance of about a mile when, having passed Stratford Bridge, it curved to the north and, crossing the valley of the River Chew, followed along the western side of that stream to Chew Stoke.

On leaving that place the line continued up the valley to Chew Magna, where, after turning to the eastward it crossed the main street at the southern end of the village, and reached the higher ground on the southern side of the Chew Valley. After running parallel to the Chelwood Road it passed a little to the north of Bromley Colliery and thence, turning to the north east, formed a junction with the North Somerset branch of the Great Western Railway at the southern end of Pensford Viaduct.

It was proposed to provide stations or stopping places at Blagdon, Ubley, and near the Blue Bowl Inn, to serve Compton Martin and East and West Harptree; at Sutton Wick, Chew Stoke, Chew Magna and Stanton Drew. The route had been carefully selected so as to best serve local requirements, and develop the agricultural, mining and other interests in the neighbourhood.

It was proposed to apply to the Light Railway Order Commissioners for authority to construct the line under the Light Railways Act of 1896. The gauge would be standard, so as to accommodate the ordinary rolling stock of the country, enabling both passenger and goods trains to travel over it in connection with the Great Western Railway Company's system, to which it was believed it would form a valuable feeder.

Apart from the agricultural and mining traffic, there was no doubt that the district, being close to the city of Bristol would soon develop a fine residential traffic. The building of the line could be expeditiously carried out, and a good return upon the capital outlay could be confidently relied upon.

An alternative and more direct route had also been examined, leaving the line described at Stratford Bridge, and running to the east of Bishop Sutton, it took up the line of route first described. If that route were adopted it would effect a saving of about 1½ miles in the distance between Blagdon and Pensford, and from £18,000 to £20,000 in the cost of construction; but it should be noted that neither Chew Stoke nor Chew Magna would then secure the advantages of railway communication.

In reply to questions it was stated that the probable cost of obtaining the Bill would be about £1,000 and the railway would be in working order in two years after obtaining the order.

All public roads, except two, were to be crossed on the level. The Prospectus promised tourist traffic, for in the early 20th century many urban dwellers were keen to go into the countryside at weekends and summer evenings. Bromley Colliery's mining engineer said that 600 acres of coal was available to be worked and most of the present output of 15,000 tons per annum had to be taken to Pensford station by cart or traction engine. He promised that if the line was built, he would place at least 1,000 tons a week on it.

County councillor G.N. Armstrong successfully moved a resolution that an application be made to the Light Railway Commissioners for a Light Railway Order to build the Blagdon & Pensford Light Railway.

On 11th July, 1905 the Commissioners held an enquiry at the Pelican Hotel, Chew Magna under the chairmanship of the Hon. A.E. Gathorne-Hardy and an Order was subsequently granted on 20th March, 1906. Despite early enthusiasm, the company received insufficient backing, so coal from Pensford and Bromley never travelled direct by rail to Blagdon pumping station.

The North Somerset Light Railway

In the mid-1950s, two Bristol businessmen, S. Jones-Frank and Major W.D.I. Gunn, founded the North Somerset Light Railway Company Limited, with offices at 57 Queen Square, Bristol. They hoped to rebuild the Weston, Clevedon & Portishead Light Railway between Worle and Clevedon using a gauge of 2 ft 8 in. There was to be a half-mile diversion from the Light Railway's roadbed at the Clevedon end in order to reach Salthouse Fields near the sea front. *Septimus*, a 0-4-2ST which had hitherto worked on Pike's Tramway at Furzebrook in Dorset, was returned to its makers, Peckett & Company of Bristol, for overhaul and fitting of the vacuum brake for use on the relaid line. The project did not reach the practical stage as only a new Act of Parliament could overcome the complicated legal position of the old Weston, Clevedon & Portishead Light Railway and allow the new one to purchase the trackbed.

Stymied, Frank and Gunn looked elsewhere in the vicinity and in 1956 were offered the roadbed from Langford to Blagdon, complete with station buildings, bridges, etc. for £1,200. Unfortunately they were unable to proceed before the acceptance date expired and plans were abandoned. *Septimus* was scrapped by Joseph Pugsley at Peckett's in 1962.

Bibliography

Books

An Historical Survey of Selected Great Western Stations by R.H. Clark (OPC, 1976)
Clinker's Register of Closed Passenger Stations & Goods Depots by C.R. Clinker (Avon-Anglia, 1988)
The Railway at Congresbury by the Congresbury History Group (1986)
Track Layout Diagrams of the GWR and BR/WR, Section 15: Taunton and West Somerset by R.A. Cooke (Author, 1990)
The Wrington Vale Light Railway by M. Farr, C.G. Maggs, R. Lovell & C. Whetmath (Avon-Anglia, 1978)
Industrial Locomotives of South West England (Industrial Railway Society, 1977)
Great Western Engine Sheds 1837-1947 by E. Lyons & E. Mountford (OPC, 1979)
Branch Line to Cheddar including the Wrington Vale Light Railway by V. Mitchell and K. Smith (Middleton Press, 1997)
Steaming Through the Cheddar Valley by D. Phillips (OPC, 2001)
Locomotives of the Great Western Railway (RCTS, 1952-1993)
Through Countryside and Coalfield by M. Vincent (OPC, 1990)
Great Western Branch Line Modelling Parts 1 & 2 by S. Williams (Wild Swan, 1991)

Magazines and Newspapers

Bath Chronicle
British Railway Journal
Clevedon Mercury
Engineering
Bristol Evening Post
Great Western Railway Journal
Great Western Railway Magazine
Model Railway News
Railway Magazine
Railway Modeller
Railway Times
Western Daily Press
Weston Gazette
Weston Mercury

Acknowledgements

I would like to thank A. Bond, R. Day, M.E.J. Deane, M. Farr, W.G. Gait, A. Maslen, C. Warburton, and M. Wathen. Especial thanks are due to John Hayward and Colin Roberts for checking and improving the text. While working for the GWR in pre-World War II days, John Hayward travelled over the branch in a special train conveying a loaded horse box.

Index

Compare this view of Langford station taken on 23rd August, 1954 with the one on page 54, taken just four years earlier, and see how quickly the railway is losing its battle against nature. *Author*